THE NEW NO-NONSENSE CONSTITUTION OF THE UNITED STATES OF AMERICA

THE FANTASY OF THE 21ST CENTURY

Dr. Alex Blaivas

THE NEW NO-NONSENCE CONSTITUTION OF THE UNITED STATES OF AMERICA

THE FANTASY OF THE 21ST CENTURY

Preamble Note

As divined in the year 1788, the Constitution of the United States is now almost 250 years old. Written in archaic English, it covers only a fraction of contemporary situations. In the meantime, many changes in society and technology have taken place, and many propositions thereof now appear outdated. The Amendments to the Constitution haven't been able to remedy many problems which have led to instability in American Society. The text below provides a new edition of the American Constitution.

1 DEFINITIONS AND INTRODUCTION

1.1 The United States Economic Reality

1.1.1 The backbone of every economic system are people. People are born unequal. They are divided in races and ethnicities with different biological, physical and intellectual qualities observed in every ethnicity and every race. Claims of people's equality are patently incorrect. The immutable economic system of the United States is the time-honored Free Enterprise, Capitalist System with unshakable respect for private property of law-abiding citizens, competition to survive in the marketplace and the stock market. Socialized, government sponsored medicine is not a part of the United States society and could never be advocated for the whole country, although a fraction thereof is offered as an option to the military servicemen and veterans.

1.1 Some people have roots in this country

1.2.1 Individuals with roots in this country are those who were born in the United States, lived here at least half of their lives, whose children, parents and grandparents were born in the USA, whose in-laws were likewise born in the USA down to the first generation, considering the individuals themselves being the third generation. All members of their extended family must be either their blood relatives or in-laws with roots in this country. Adoptions must only be within the family. Spending time in U.S. military units overseas is equated to living in the USA. An additional requirement for people with roots in this country is the history of no felony convictions for themselves and their families and in-laws in the span of three generations. Descendants of Illegal Immigrants cannot have roots in this country. Muslims cannot have roots in this country under any circumstances. Individuals who were adopted and whose true family history is unknown cannot have roots in this country and cannot be part of any family tree.

1.3 People occupying positions of responsibility must have documented intelligence (Intelligence Quotient - IQ) measured.

1.3.1 Individuals occupying positions of board members, teachers in high schools and university professors command positions in the Army and security forces, managers at production facilities of various kinds, managers of service clusters, e.g., airports, etc. must have documented Intelligence Quotient (IQ) 105 or above. Their IQs must be tested and verified by qualified individuals (psychologists) with a 4-year college in their background and verified IQ of at least 110. Their certificates must be displayed in the offices where they practice.

1.3.2 Large companies might establish their own laboratories to test the IQ of their staff and new applicants for jobs. All IQs individually determined must be stored in All-American database accessible to all researchers but not to the general public. The companies also might establish their own levels of threshold IQ, however in such cases the threshold IQ cannot be less than 105.

1.3.3 All lawyers practicing on county, state and Federal levels must have a documented IQ of at least 115. Judges on all levels must have an IQ of at least 125. They also must have roots in this country. Lawyers practicing in the United States are prohibited from acquiring titles of distinction e.g., "Best lawyer in America" or similar. They are allowed to advertise the number of cases they have won and how many they've lost. They can do it on a single Internet page allotted to them.

1.4 Scientific Knowledge Requirement for Public Officials

1.4.1 Individuals applying for public offices on State and Federal levels must certify their personal understanding and acceptance of basic scientific facts articulated in this Constitution (section **36.1, Addendum II**) and must pass a series of tests (section **46, Appendix**) confirming their ability to interpret the reality that surrounds us from the scientific point of view. Lawyers applying for elective or assigned legal positions are exempt from this requirement. Lawyers cannot be considered for running for any non-judicial positions on County, State and Federal levels.

1.5 Individuals with Special Attributes.

Voting privilege and procedures.

1.5.1 Suffrage in the United States is NOT universal. It is a privilege given to the sector of the population deemed to be the backbone of our country historically, known for their low criminality, contributing to the country's prosperity intellectually and to the nation defense. Each state must be divided into zones, not necessarily contiguous, based on the average values of the dwellings located therein. The zones, where individual homes/apartments/condominiums have average values below 30% of the average value of the same in the entire state, are not allowed to vote for candidates for any position. Explicitly, they are not allowed to take part in County, State and U.S. Federal elections, they cannot run for a position of a mayor and cannot vote for the candidates of the above. Non-voting zones are characterized by individual, families and groups displaying high rate of crime, attacks on retail establishments, destruction of cultural monuments, residents depending on social assistance, and riots. The state legislatures might change this threshold depending on local ethnography in the range of 5-40%.

1.5.2 Residents of non-voting zones are not allowed to purchase and own firearms. Their firearms if suspected must be extracted possibly by force. If non-voting zones are also high crime zones, they might be at least partially fenced off with barbed wire and a single entrance gate. For the urban barbed wire fence to be erected, an order from the Secretary of the Department of Homeland Security is needed. The funds for the fence construction and maintenance must be allotted by the U.S. Congress in an annual budget. Adequate security for the fence must be provided by local authorities and the police are responsible for their stability and long-term survival. Destruction or breaching of an erected fence is punishable by 15 years in prison. This fact must be advertised with large placards positioned on or near the fence itself. Electronic monitoring equipment must be used to safeguard the fence system. Fences with a history of frequent episodes of damage or destruction might be electrified with high voltage.

1.5.3 Those who move from a voting zone to a non-voting zone or vice versa must either deregister or register for voting, depending on the direction of the move. The age of the voting privilege begins at 21 years for men and women. Registration for voting requires presenting a photo ID, taking fingerprints and a personal photograph on the spot and signature collection. Facial visual recognition and other biometric techniques must also be applied. Nobody is allowed to vote in any election without these necessary prerequisites.

1.5.4 At the time of registration for voting, the individuals must declare their party affiliation (Republicans or Democrats) for subsequent participation in the partisan primary process. Switching party affiliation is allowed but not within six months of the primaries for the next election for the party the individual wants to switch to.

1.5.5 Voting during the general election is mandatory for inhabitants of voting zones and avoidance is punishable by an annual Federal and State Tax surcharges in the amount of 2%. Reservations for American Indians are all considered voting zones. The requirement of mandatory voting is waived for them. Any farm owner, their families and farm workers are considered living in voting zones. In any case, they must be American Citizens and meet all other requirements to vote.

1.5.6 The allocation of the voting/non-voting zones is the responsibility of state legislatures and must be reflected in the National Census conducted every year divisible by 10 and thus ending with a zero. Maps of voting and non-voting zones must be published by Internet search companies and become accessible to everyone three months after this Constitution is enacted. In case the local legislations are unable or unwilling to define the voting/nonvoting zones, this responsibility must be taken by the Federal Government on a temporary basis.

1.5.7 Eligible voters must be registered in corresponding voting zones, and are thereby called "Registered Voters." They can register in only one Voting Zone in the Country. Registration must occur no later than two weeks prior to any election for the individual to be able to vote in a forthcoming election. Voters registered as affiliated with the Republican Party are allowed to vote only in Republican Primaries as well as only voters registered as affiliated with the Democratic Party are allowed to vote only in Democratic Primaries. Voting in primaries is NOT mandatory. During General Elections any registered voter can vote for either of the two parties.

1.5.8 For individuals living in non-voting zones, no criminal or civil litigation can be initiated on their behalf. Any such lawsuits must be dismissed immediately.
No caucuses are allowed in primaries. All voting must be done by casting paper ballots with electronic control with the final results announced publicly, but individual votes must be kept confidential forever.

1.5.9 In the event of death of a person living in a Voting Zone, or their relocation into a nursing or group home, the local city or county council must notify the state's election commission in order that such person might be taken off of the voting rolls.

1.5.10 Followers of prophet Mohammed, Muslims, are considered living in a special non-voting zone. No criminal or civil litigation can be initiated on their behalf. They are therefore prohibited from joining any political party. Giving political asylum to Muslims is prohibited. Homeless population does not vote, they are considered living in a special non-voting zone with zero value of their homes, and no criminal or civil litigation can be initiated on their behalf. Illegal immigrants or their descendants do not vote and are not protected by law. Those who have no right to vote also are forbidden from running for seats in any legislative body in the United States or Attorneys General offices. Suspects in pretrial detention in jails do not vote. Convicted prisoners residing in state or federal prisons are prohibited from voting while in prisons as well as after their release from prisons for the rest of their lives.

1.5.11 Residents of the nursing, group homes, assisted living homes, residents of subsidized housings are prohibited from voting even if they are located in voting zones. Such buildings where they reside are excluded from being used for calculating the average value of dwellings in their neighborhoods or the entire state. Jails and prisons as well as industrial or healthcare companies' buildings are likewise excluded from calculating the average value of the area dwellings. In short, only bona fide structures, potentially used for living on a long-term basis by individuals, those that constitute a property value for their owners are included in calculations.

1.5.12 The voting age begins at 21, which is also the age when people can legally purchase alcohol in the Entire United States. Individuals older than 65 must obtain and present a medical certificate from their primary physicians, of competency to vote or a freshly documented Intelligence

Quotient no less than 95. Individuals falling below this threshold are excused from voting. Individuals presenting an IQ certificate which is less than 95 are not required to be retested in the future, however if their IQ is 95 or greater at any given time, they must be retested every four years.

1.5.13 All individuals living temporarily in convalescent homes, hospitalized at medical facilities on a temporary basis are relieved from obligation to vote for a period of their hospitalization. The voting booths cannot leave the designated place for voting where the majority of the population votes on Election Day. Portable voting boxes are condemned and prohibited. Voting on the Election Day for every individual must begin with a ritual of complete personal identification which must include presentation of the photo ID and using biometric features. Advertisement for any candidate is prohibited on Election Day and three days prior to the election.

1.5.14 Members of the United States Armed Forces, members of State National Guard units, as well as military veterans, *free of felony convictions*, are all symbolically located in a voting zone whether they are positioned in the United States or overseas. Subject to age restriction they must vote in Presidential Elections only if they are stationed overseas, and in Presidential, State and local elections in case they are situated in the United States, regardless of the location of their individual dwellings. Upon retirement they keep all such privileges intact. Their family members also have similar privilege. Independent contractors hired by the Department of Defense or CIA for special tasks are considered living in voting zones under all circumstances while overseas on assignments but might be excused from voting, depending on their operational status overseas. Individuals serving in Law Enforcement and other security establishments, their families are all considered living in voting zones individually, as long as they are employed there, and after their honorable retirement, although their next-door neighbors may never vote if the location is in a non-voting zone overall. Families of individuals fallen in the line of duty in the police force retain the voting privilege for the rest of their individual lives.

1.5.15 Expatriates living overseas on a permanent basis vote only in case if they keep the American citizenship. They vote in American Embassies and Consulates of respective countries. Had they fallen in a non-voting category for reasons described above if they instead were living in the USA, they do not vote.

1.5.16 Individuals with at least one felony conviction are forbidden from voting in any election for the rest of their lives. They are forbidden from endorsing a candidate or campaigning for or against one. When people apply for registration in a voting zone, the staff must check their names and social security numbers against a database of individuals with criminal convictions. In case of a positive identification, their applications are rejected. They are then relieved from having a 2% tax surcharge for not voting.

1.5.17 Any dishonest manipulation of the electoral process, with intent to give unlawful advantage to either party, is a prosecutable offense; those include voting more than once, casting a vote not for themselves but for someone else, buying votes, destroying the voting database or parts thereof, and facilitation of relaxation of registration procedures for the sake of falsification of the voting process. The punishment for violating these legal pillars is 10 years in prison.

1.5.18 All elective positions require the applicants to have roots in this country. All judges, attorneys and attorneys general positions, elected or assigned must be filled only by people with roots in this country.

1.5.19 For the potential candidates for positions on State and lower levels, their parents and grandparents, their offspring, as well as their in-laws on the same levels an additional requirement of not being associated with companies involved in local urban or countrywide urban or industrial development must be satisfied. The mental orientation of all elected officials must be that of the protection of the environment, nature, wildlife, flora and fauna of the regions, supporting acts to counteract the global warming, gradual diminution of usage of fossil fuels, prevention of forest fires and irrigation of dry lands.

1.5.20 All voting, for one third of the State Senates and all State Houses of Representatives candidates, U.S. House of Representatives, and one third of the U.S. Senate, must be performed in one day which is the first Tuesday of November of even years (from 8:00 a.m. to 8:00 p.m.) and all voting for President, Vice-President, Governors and Lieutenant Governors must be performed on the same day in November of every leap year in the same time window. Elections on a County and lower levels (if available) must adjust to this schedule. A police post must be established at every voting place. Earlier voting is not allowed. Security cordons must be established around each voting place with cement blocks to prevent vehicular attacks.

1.5.21 Absentee ballots must be received by the voting commission with USPS date stamping, no later than two days before the in-person voting. All envelopes with absentee ballots must be opened and counted on the Election Day. Absentee ballots may be sent to absentee voters only upon receiving their written and signed request with signatures notarized. A valid reason must accompany every absentee ballot request. Their email address must be a part of the application for notification, whether the application has been accepted or rejected. The total number of absentee ballots in every jurisdiction cannot exceed 0.2% of all ballots cast in person. Every absentee vote must be signed and the signature notarized before mailing. The signatures must be explicitly legible. Illegible signatures are rejected.

1.5.22 All elective positions, with the exception of judicial positions which are nonpartisan, might be sought only by members of either Republican or Democratic parties provided they meet the aforementioned criteria. Other parties might be formed but their members are never allowed to register candidates for any election. The candidates must be the winners of primaries of their respective parties (Republicans or Democrats). Running for a position as an Independent is not allowed although attorneys always run as an independent for their judicial positions. Their candidacies must be officially endorsed by their corresponding bar associations. Multiple judicial candidates can be endorsed for running for the same judicial position.

1.5.23 Governors and Lieutenant Governors of all states of the Union are elected on the first Tuesday of November of the leap year for a four-year term. If reelected at the end of this term they have an option to serve another four years which must be final for them, thus in case of being reelected they would have served eight years in aggregate which is the maximum time allowed for them to serve in this office. In case they lose the reelection bid at the end of their first four-year term, they cannot run for reelection again in that state. They must have lived in that state for seven years before attempting to get elected as the Governor or Lieutenant Governor. They must have an IQ of at least 125, have graduated from a four-year college, (with the exception of a law school) and have passed all scientific tests required by this constitution. They also must have roots in this country.

1.5.24 Mayors of U.S. municipalities are elected on the first Tuesday of November of even years in order to serve two years, must have roots in this country, to have lived in that municipality for seven years or more, have an IQ of at least 115 and a history of graduating from a four-year college with the exception of a law school.

1.5.25 Candidates for County and State level offices must have resided at least seven years in corresponding jurisdictions in a voting zone. Candidates for U.S. Senate and House of Representatives must have resided at least seven years in corresponding states in their voting zones.

1.5.26 It is acceptable for the U.S. Department of Homeland Security to monitor electronic communications of non-voting individuals living in the United States without explicit permission of the judge.

1.5.27 Individual voters must spend no more than five minutes in the voting booth when they have a possession of the voting ballot. Their actual time must be counted and should they exceed the time limit, they should be removed and counted as non-voting. If the ballot is dropped in the ballot box with some positions unchecked, those positions are ignored.

1.5.28 The New Constitution relies heavily on new technology and strict description of protocols, which make errors or falsification of voting results impossible.

Therefore, claims of incorrect results are prohibited. The losing party must always accept defeat without questioning. Voting recounts are prohibited.

1.6 Extraordinary situations

1.6.1 Devastating fires, floods, hurricanes might destroy the individuals' dwellings and put residents in situation of uncertainty. They are still considered living in voting zones for up to 18 months after the disaster, if they lived there before the calamity, and in non-voting zones otherwise.

1.6.2 No situation, no matter how grave, warrants declaration of the Martial Law in the United States. However, in cases of groups of individuals creating obstacles to transportation and flow of goods over the landmass or in the port entries to the United States, an emergency regime might be declared by the President for a short time of 10 days to clear the obstacles. This emergency regime cannot be extended and such declaration is allowed only once a year. If motor vehicles are involved in illegal blockage of normal traffic, the government will possess the power to seal off the area, arrest the organizers, tow away illegally parked trucks and other vehicles. The participants might be arrested and charged with disorderly conduct; their driver licenses suspended. Their bank accounts might be frozen. In case of crane operators deliberately slowing loading/unloading operations at the U.S. ports of entry their firing might resolve the problem quickly. Temporarily, the cranes might then be entrusted for operation to the managers of the port facilities. Hiring new crane operators and training them will resolve the problem expediently.

1.6.3 The USA streets must be free of makeshift constructions erected by the homeless. Building homeless shelters is prohibited. Relocating homeless individuals to voting areas, swanky, elite neighborhoods, and housing them there is prohibited and punishable by 15 years in prison. Public funds cannot be used for homeless' healthcare. Violation carries a punishment of four years in prison.

1.7 Public Procurement Market

1.7.1 Only American, Canadian, British, German, Japanese, South Korean, Australian and New Zeeland companies can participate in bidding for projects offered via the Public Procurement. Procurement for military and security projects must be reserved for American companies only. The companies participating in public procurement must prove that they are not controlled by communist or totalitarian/authoritarian countries and don't have electronic devices in equipment installed in the USA manufactured in communist or generally hostile countries.

1.7.2 The fence at the American-Mexican border is an integral part of the United States, part of the country's security and must be completed and maintained. Attempts to invalidate the idea of the US-Mexican border fence is punishable by 25 years in prison.

1.8 Issues out of scope of any legislative power in the United States.

1.8.1 Wealth redistribution by the government, creation of a welfare state, nationalization of industries or healthcare systems are both condemned and prohibited. Creating entitlement programs is prohibited. Segregated primary, middle and high school systems are the reflection of the current reality. They are allowed. Their existence cannot be challenged. Busing children from poor neighborhoods to schools in the neighborhoods with higher individual incomes or vice versa is condemned and prohibited. This practice that has deserved the highest condemnation proved a total failure due to ignorance of racial and ethnic attributes by liberal stalwarts of the United States. Enforcing creation and maintenance of gender-neutral departments in stores for kids is prohibited. Abortions are out of scope of any legislative initiative; abortions are explicitly allowed and cannot be restricted or banned. Pills to terminate pregnancy cannot be restricted or banned. Existence of the Family Planning clinics (planned parenthood) must be encouraged and protected by the courts and legislations. There will be no reparations for slavery.

I.8.2 Transgender girls are not allowed to participate in girls' competitions in school and elsewhere and subsequently in women's competitions. Transgender boys are forbidden from serving in the Armed Forces of the United States. Non-Union workers are prohibited from paying union dues. Union accounts must be frozen if they violate this rule. Maintenance of elementary, middle and high schools is the responsibility of the local communities, whose children attend those schools, through local taxes. Government subsidies are allowed only for schools where every student has an IQ of 95 or more. American Indian schools (on reservations) are exempt from this requirement. Indigenous people have a veto power over urban or industrial development in their areas. Gender is assigned at birth. It is either male or female. In rare cases of biological ambiguity, the obstetrician or a midwife makes a decision based on their individual practice or in consultation with other specialists. It is prohibited to spend public funds on gender identity conversion or treating homeless in public or private hospitals at public expense.

Patent waivers are prohibited. They undermine integrity of the patent system and are equivalent to the infringement.

1.8.3 Gig workers are not employees. They are independent contractors, they cannot unionize.

1.9 BASIC AMERICAN RIGHTS
(Pertaining to U.S. citizens, living in voting zones only)

1.9.1 Right of Free Speech expressed verbally, or in a written form, perhaps in cartoons, in electronic media (Internet) or in cinematography, without fear of censure or condemnation, without being forced to retrieve the statements under the threat of material losses in one's business or profession, or losing a job. Sexually explicit material, pornography, especially child pornography, demands to defund the police are not a part of free speech. Islamic discourse is always full of hatred and is not free speech.

1.9.2 Right to earn a living, but not a right for a job (employment guarantee is not an issue here). Business owners whose businesses are serving the public, have a right to exclude certain segments of the population they do not like based on economic or other considerations.

1.9.3 Right to protect one's home and one's neighborhood from intruders, homeless, squatters, transients, and beggars, as well as people one does not want to live in proximity with. Squatters' cases are criminal cases, Adverse possession is a crime punishable by two years in prison. Individuals whose presence in a neighborhood might diminish the property value of a number of dwellings, might be denied residence upon the demands of 20% of a quarter a mile radius of neighborhood residents. This pertains newcomers as well as established residents who for whatever reason make other neighbors' life in the neighborhood too difficult to bear. Such rejections cannot be challenged in the court of law. The extension of this rule is the right and obligation to protect the US-Mexico border by volunteers who cannot be prosecuted for their action under any circumstances. Defenders of the US-Mexico border are granted complete legal immunity from prosecution for their actions in confrontations with the intruders trying to violate the border.

1.9.4 Residents of a recognizable neighborhood, which in some circumstances might be a single multi-story building, have a right to protest and block additional developments in their vicinity which might decrease their property values, preferred view or neighborhood security.

1.9.5 American citizens have a right to be protected against political correctness and have a right to be politically incorrect. Yes, political correctness is a part of free speech and cannot be censured, however, political incorrectness is another part of the equation and is also a part of free speech. Retribution for "politically incorrect" statements is a crime punishable by five years in prison.

1.9.6 The right of assembly, association for whatever reason, with the exception of criminal intent, permanent or temporary, to promote an agenda or simply for entertainment purposes are allowed by this Constitution. Individuals forming such associations, as long as they are located in voting zones and the individuals themselves reside in voting zones, have the right to exclude other individuals they do not like, according to their bylaws. Their bylaws have the paramount power should any membership dispute arise.

1.9.7 The New American Constitution accepts the Second Amendment to the Constitution of 1788 only for the voting population of the United States. Non-voting population is forbidden from owning firearms. Assault rifles might be sold only to property owners such as for instance gas stations, small or large shops. However, assault rifles cannot be sold to individuals younger than 25. Selling assault rifles to the general population is forbidden. All weapons sold to the public must be federally registered. Selling unmarked weapons without serial numbers and the sign of a maker, is prohibited. It is prohibited for unlicensed individuals to manufacture firearms with 3-D printers. In general, it is prohibited to manufacture firearms not detectable by the metal detectors. The gun manufacturers as well as gun retailers are free from liability for any death or violence resulting from their products provided, they follow the law. Handguns might be sold to people between 18 and 25 but they must be cleared by a psychiatrist. Gun owners must carry umbrella insurance in one million dollars in 2020 money. Selling guns to anyone without evidence of such insurance is prohibited. Individuals living within 30 miles of US-Mexican border in rural setting can own assault rifles.

1.9.8 American business owners as well as security guards protecting properties have an unalienable right to defend their businesses, and the portions of the streets they are facing, from intruders, rioters, vagabonds, robbers, beggars and shoplifters. The means of defense or break-in prevention is their choice in every case. Protection of good neighborhoods against attackers might be done by firearms defense. Individuals protecting their real estate property are automatically given absolute immunity on the spot against civilian and criminal lawsuits.

1.9.9 Confronting shoplifters is mandatory for the shop/ store owners, security guards and clerks. Allowing violators to steal merchandise fuels inflation and creates a tax imposed on the rest of the population and creates a liability for the store owners. Negligence in maintaining the integrity of the retail establishment is a crime punishable by two years in prison. Degrading lives of criminals attacking properties, by using firearms is a responsibility of store owners and such actions immediately impose protection against any liability on them.

1.9.10 Individual property owners, as well as renters have a right to defend themselves and their families with firearms against break-ins.

1.9.11 With the exception of child pornography, no book, radiobroadcast, article in a periodical or a motion picture can be banned in the United States. Children libraries in schools are a case of exception. Their contents are controlled by school boards and the students' parents.

STRUCTURE OF THE GOVERNING BODIES

2 - The Legislative Branch
2.1 - Legislature and Elections

2.1.1 All Legislative Powers in the USA are vested in the Congress of the United States, which consists of the Senate and House of Representatives. State Senates and Houses of Representatives have jurisdiction in the scope of the territories of their states in the matters not resolved by decisions of the United States Congress.

2.1.2 Lawyers are prohibited from becoming legislators. Neither the members of the U.S. Senate nor the U.S. House of Representative nor members of the State Houses of Representatives or Senates could be lawyers.

2.1.2 - The United States House of Representatives

2.2.1 The U.S. House of Representatives shall be composed of members chosen every even year by the Registered Voters of all States. The states' houses of representatives shall consist of members that have been chosen by registered voters of the corresponding individual states.

2.2.2 Each State shall have at least one U.S. Representative, while the total size of a state's delegation to the U.S. House depends on their number of registered votes. The total number of members in the U.S. House of Representatives must be 200.

2.2.3 The number of members of the U.S. House of Representatives apportioned to each state is determined as follows. For at least one year before each Federal Election (the first Tuesday of November of odd years), the States report to the Federal Election Commission the number of registered votes in their corresponding states. The Commission then adds them all up and divides this number by 200 thus receiving the number of registered voters that will eventually vote for or against a single representative. The total number of each state's registered votes is then divided by this number with the result that is the total number of representatives each state sends to the Congress. Fractions are rounded up. The Commission then informs every state of their number of Representatives for the next two-year period. Each Representative can serve only 12 years in aggregate, not necessarily continuously, during their lifetime. Each Representative will have one vote.

2.2.4 Any person running for a seat on this legislative body, as well as individual states' Houses of Representatives must have attained the age of twenty-five years, to have been an inhabitant of the state where they hope to be elected for at least seven years, and have roots in this country. They cannot be lawyers in their profession and must have a documented IQ of at least 125. They also must have passed a set of scientific tests before the first attempt to be elected. The candidates might run for election between the ages 25 and 68. Passage of all scientific tests is mandatory for candidates running for a place in the U.S. House of Representatives and the State Houses of Representatives.

2.2.5 The House of Representatives will choose their speaker and other Officers. Special elections outside of regular elections in November of the even years are not allowed for the House of Representatives of the U.S. Congress. The United States House of Representatives has a sole power of Impeachment, which is indictment of the high-level public officials. The concurrence of a simple majority of delegates in the House is required for impeachment and all delegates' votes must be kept forever secret, all electronic or paper records destroyed, only the totals made public. Distribution of the votes along the party lines must also be kept secret.

2.2.6 On the floor of the U.S. House of Representatives no speech can last longer than 30 minutes. This rule is also applicable to the states' houses of representatives.

2.2.7 Members of any legislature in the United States, their relatives and in-laws are forbidden from trading in the stock market.

2.3 - The United States Senate

2.3.1 The Senate of the United States must be composed of two Senators from each State. Each senator will serve a term of six years; and each Senator shall have one vote.

2.3.2 One third of the Senate must be terminated every two years with their seats being opened for a new election. Each Senator can serve only 12 years in aggregate in the Senate, not necessarily continuously, during their lifetime. The requirements for a Senator include: being a citizen of the United States with roots in this country, at least a four-year college education with the exception of a law school, IQ of at least 125, and aged between 25 and 70 years. No candidate can be elected to serve as a Senator if they are older than 64 years. Passage of all scientific tests is mandatory for the prospective senators.

2.3.3 The Vice President of the United States must be the President of the U.S. Senate, but will have no vote, unless the vote for a particular item equally divides the Senate chamber (a tie). The Vice-President, however, cannot vote for the Impeachment of the President as well as when the subject of Impeachment is the Vice-President themselves (see also 2.3.5).

2.3.4 The Senate shall choose their other Officers, and also a President of the Senate *pro tempore,* in the absence of the Vice President, or when he shall exercise the Office of President of the United States.

2.3.5 The Senate shall have the sole Power to try all Impeachments of the high-level public officials, that is to try individuals indicted (impeached) by the House of Representatives with the results that might be either acquittal or found guilty. When sitting for that purpose, they shall be on Oath or Affirmation. If and when the President of the United States is tried, the Chief Justice shall preside, the Chief Justice also votes; and no Person shall be convicted without the concurrence of two thirds of the Senate members. All votes cast by individual senators, as well as by the Chief Justice, must be kept secret forever, all electronic or paper records destroyed, only the total is revealed during the session. Distribution of the votes along the party lines must also be kept forever secret. The same rule is valid for voting on personnel matters when it comes to voting to confirm the heads of the departments, ambassadors, and other high-level officials. Voting on personnel matters, other than impeachments, pertains to the Senate only. If an impeached President is tried in the Senate and found guilty, the Secret Service removes this President from the White House immediately. A special Commission is then formed to review the content of the President's documents in the Oval Office and make sure that no secret documents will go with the President into his place of retirement. The Vice President then assumes the role of President.

2.3.6 Punishment in Cases of Impeachment is removal from Office, and disqualification to hold and enjoy any Office of Honor forever, but the Party convicted shall nevertheless be liable and subject to Indictment by a Grand Jury, Trial, Judgment and Punishment by an independent court according to Law. The same rules must be applied to the Impeachment of the Vice President and the President if the situation arises.

2.3.7 Every legislator in the House and the Senate as well as the President must sign a statement that they have read every word in upcoming bills, that they voted for or against, in physical time allotted to them. Without it the bill cannot become law.

2.3.8 In case of death or incapacitation of a Senator, with their term expiring longer than one year after the event, a special election is held to fill the vacancy. Such special elections must be done on the first Tuesday of November of even years. In the meantime, while waiting for the election, the late senator's spouse might take the position.

2.3.9 On the floor of the Senate no speech can last longer than 30 minutes. This rule is applicable to the States' Senates as well.

2.3.10 The responsibility of the Senate is to observe the New Constitution, provide sufficient financial support to the U.S. Armed Forces, the U.S. economy, and the U.S. position in the World.

3 EXECUTIVE BRANCH

3.1 PRESIDENT AND VICE PRESIDENT OF THE UNITED STATES

3.1.1 At the beginning of the Presidential Campaigns, presidential candidates, as well as candidates for vice-president, for both parties must take an MMPI-2 Restructured Form (MMPI-2-RF) test which is Minnesota Multiphasic Personality Inventory presented by a qualified mental health professional, and the results must be properly documented and made public. MMPI is a single life-time only test; in case the same individual appears in similar circumstances again, no additional MMPI testing is needed. Only the interpretive conclusions of individual's MMPI tests must be made public and available to all party members before the primary vote of the corresponding party. Specific answers, however, must be kept secret forever. Primary voting must be always secret, the cumulative results only are announced without mentioning the names of the individual party members who stand behind the primary votes.

3.1.2 The President, other elected and assigned officials must expect to be possibly subjected to public criticism which is a gold tradition of American Democracy. Whistleblowing is another form of criticism and must be protected. Any attempt on retaliation is considered unpatriotic, antisocial and might be prosecuted. Dissent must be protected.

President as well as Vice-President both are prohibited from giving orders to the Secret Service of the United States. President is not a commander of the Secret Service. All communications of this nature must be done through a special commission of the Congress consisting of four Senators (two Democrats and two Republicans) and four members of the House of Representatives (also two Democrats and two Republicans). This commission is vested with the command of the Secret Service.

3.1.3 ELECTORAL College

Electoral College exists to elect the U.S. President and Vice-President indirectly based on votes cast by the voting part of the population. Each state sends the number of electors to the Electoral College equal to the number of their representatives in the House of Representatives of the United States Congress plus their two U.S. senators. The electors are partisan by definition, e.g., if a particular state has overwhelmingly voted for one party during a presidential election, then all electors from this state must represent this party. The electors are calculated based on simple majority -- winner takes all, in all 50 states.

3.1.4 If the voting population of a particular state is split equally to a single person between two parties, this state does not send any electors to the electoral college. Residents of the District of Columbia (Washington DC) do not send any representatives to the Electoral College. The voting residents of D.C. vote in local elections only. The Electoral College convenes six weeks after the day of the Election. They are given eight hours to cast their votes. The electors thus elect the President and Vice President of the United States by casting their votes. The winner must be elected by absolute majority, however, if after one attempt no winner emerges, the winner then is determined by a simple majority. The electors must cast their votes for candidates who are the winners of the popular vote in their respective states. The votes cast by the electors could not be secret. Attempts to replace the legitimate electors by people who might sway the choice of the election officials is a crime punishable by 25 years in prison.

3.1.5 The place where Electoral college convenes is Dover, Delaware, United States. Any state might send two observers, one Republican, one Democrat. They must be provided with corresponding badges with their name and states they represent clearly visible. The observers must be provided with a detail description of the procedure and necessary comments. The observers are obligated to be absolutely neutral during the work of the Electoral College and never try to influence the election in any way. The violation of this rule is a crime punishable by five years in prison.

3.1.6 The Chief Justice of the Supreme Court announces the winner in the vote in the Electoral College in a session of Congress on the first business Wednesday in January of the year following the leap election year. The defeated party is prohibited from claiming fraud once the announcement is made.

3.1.7 The Inauguration of the President and Vice-President takes place on the 3rd Wednesday of January of the year following the leap year. The outgoing President and the incoming one are given 30 minutes each to make speeches.

3.1.8 The President and Vice-President must be models of honesty, integrity, and dedication to the office. Both candidates for President and Vice-President must disclose their financial status, the Federal, state and local taxes, they have paid for the preceding five years before the primary voting of their respective parties. The financial disclosure must be made four months before the primary voting. Unless they did so before voting, their names are forbidden from entering the voting rolls in their corresponding primaries. They must avoid getting engaged in personal feuds and speak malevolently about their opponents. The President is compensated at the rate of tenfold average annual salary of the U.S. workers, and vice-president at the rate of eightfold thereof.

3.1.9 President is forbidden from pardoning himself, members of his cabinet, their relations, personal friends, individuals who donated any sums of money to their election campaign, or their family members and in-laws, their personal lawyers as well as the same of Vice-President. The Justice Department's Clemency Office must be consulted in every case. Preemptive pardons are prohibited. Every pardon must be directed at only one specific crime which must be described. Umbrella pardons are forbidden. President is entitled to issue only 10 pardons per term. He cannot issue any pardons during the last two weeks adjacent to the end of his term even if he has been reelected. The President may serve only eight years in aggregate, with an opportunity afforded to them to seek their party nomination for the second term contiguous to the first four-year term. However, if they lose a reelection bid at the end of their first four years, they can run again in one of the subsequent elections for another four years (provided their party nominated them) which will be their final if they win a reelection bid.

3.1.10 The President (if a male) shall be the Commander in Chief of the United States Army, Air Force, Marine Corps, Space Force and the Navy of the United States, as well as the National Guard, U.S. Coast Guard, and of the Militia of the several States, when the latter are called into the actual Service of the United States. Posse Comitatus Act of 1878, updated in 1956 and 1981, is respected by this Constitution. The National Guard Units are under dual control of the Governors of the individual states and the Department of Defense. The National Guard is not covered by the Posse Comitatus. They might come under direct control of the President during exceptional circumstances for a short time of one month.

3.1.11 The President is entitled to some executive actions; however, they cannot violate the Constitution, and they must be limited to the effect of 60 days and unless approved by Congress during the aforementioned period they are inactivated. Only 10 executive actions are allowed per term. The new Constitution highly discourages any grandstanding, boastful, self-promoting, self-congratulatory statements on the part of the President or Vice-President. The Senate and the House of Representatives are encouraged to censure presidents for such behavior should it occur which is not the same as impeachment. Censure requires votes of both House and the Senate with a simple majority and the vote must be confidential with only the final result given to the public, and can be arranged only twice per a four-year Presidential term.

3.1.12 The President has a power of the line-item veto applied exclusively to the annual budget; he can exercise it no more than 20 times per budget. The President's decision to veto certain budget items cannot be challenged by the Congress which has the privilege of voting for the budget as a whole.

3.1.13 Neither the President nor any high ranking elected or assigned officials have a right to declare Martial Law. Martial law is prohibited in the United States.

3.1.14 The President as well as Vice President are prohibited from bringing relatives and in-laws to the cabinet even in the role of consultants. The President or Vice-President might be impeached by the House if either of them committed treason, bribery or other high crimes, that is, indicted by the House of Representatives and convicted by the Senate even after leaving the office within 60 days. Both President and Vice-President must keep their investments in a blind trust during their days in office. Neither President nor Vice-President once convicted by the Senate can run for any elective office in the country or international organizations in the future. The Constitution discourages future presidents from excessive travels, or otherwise taking advantage of their status of an active or retired top civilian.

3.1.15 Votes for impeachment in the House and the trial in the Senate are conducted in confidence and the individual votes are never announced. All personnel votes e.g., for the heads of the Departments are likewise kept confidential. Personnel votes are conducted in the Senate only. All other votes in the Senate and the House are not confidential and open to the public unless deemed pertaining to confidential military or security affairs.

3.1.16 The President cannot adjourn any house of Congress under any circumstances.

3.1.17 History has confirmed that the presence of U.S. troops in foreign lands guarantees at least temporary truce and stability over there. Unilateral removal of such protection might cause the situation there to tilt toward a dangerous outcome. Unilateral removal of such troops from the dangerous spots of the Globe is prohibited for the President or Vice-President and must be explicitly approved by the Congress.

3.1.18 During Inauguration, both President and Vice-President must swear that they would uphold the Constitution of the United States, never deviate from the principle of Democracy in the United States, and avoid authoritarian acts which are outside the Constitution.

3.2 - Elections, Meetings

3.2.1 Public prayers, sermons on the territory of the Washington DC Capitol, prayers and sermons in the confines of any government structure or buildings belonging to Federal or any state government are all forbidden, with the exception of the Pentagon, Military Colleges, Army, Navy, Marine Corps, Space Force, ATF, U.S. Coast Guard and the National Guard units.

3.2.2 All Representatives must run for reelection if they desire to serve further, after completing a two-year term through the voting process administered on the First Tuesday of November of even years. Representatives who lost the reelection or whose permitted term in Congress has expired, must resign on the First Business Wednesday of January of the year following the even or leap election year. Newly elected Representatives step into their new positions on the same day in January of the postelection year after they have been certified by the U.S. Election Assistance Commission.

3.2.3 In the leap year when this new Constitution is enacted, all potential senators (candidates) must run to be elected to positions in the empty chamber. Subsequently, one third of the body then must either resign after two years or run for reelection for the term of six years. The Senators who must do so, must be selected randomly by software with Random Number Generator. Next even year another third of the Senate must either resign or run for reelection for the term of six years. At the end of the sixth year since initiation of the new Senate (the next leap year) the last third of the Senate members must either resign or run for reelection.

3.2.4 At each election station, three representatives of Democrats and three representatives of Republicans are allowed to be present on the day of the Election in November of even years. On Election Day, approaching people waiting in line offering them food or drink or asking them to reveal or change their intended vote is prohibited under the penalty of two years in prison. Using blaring horns directed at the line of people waiting to cast their votes, or spreading leaflets with appeals to vote for one party, or creating any loud noise, is prohibited under the same two-year prison penalty.

Police are responsible for the smooth conduct of the elections and must remove (arrest) anyone trying to disrupt it.

3.2.5 Infrastructure and electronics used to count votes must be owned and controlled by a U.S. company and certified by the U.S. Department of Justice. Using foreign manufactured equipment is prohibited. Each even year the Election Commission must run a simple demonstration of the effectiveness and fairness of the election hardware and software one month before the election. For the demonstration, a limited number of hardware sets should randomly be elected. Between the elections the election hardware must be kept in a safe place with sufficient monitoring equipment to ensure lack of tampering. The election hardware, after being checked one month before the election must be subsequently kept near the voting stations in a safe storage area unmoved until Election Day. Three representatives of each party might be present during the testing of the election equipment. The results of monitoring must be documented in a set of affidavits.

3.2.6 All databases related to ongoing elections and their aftermath must undergo systematic back up procedure on the day of the election. The integrity of the election databases must be reviewed after each election.

3.2.7 The people who attend to the election hardware must have a background free of felonies and follow strict protocols developed by the Election Commission. Their background must be checked before each election. They also must document every stage of their handling Election Hardware electronically with the laptops or mobile phones, and be able to run comprehensive tests right before the election to determine that the software is free of malware. Right before the election the hardware must be installed by transferring it from a safe storage area. Connecting the election hardware to the Internet is prohibited until the last vote is cast. At that moment the results, computed electronically and written in an affidavit and signed by the members of the Election Staff and observers from both parties will be copied to a dedicated storage area and uploaded to the Election Commission. The signatures must be notarized by a notary public and the results made available to the States. The affidavit must be photographed by the members of the election staff. Police officers must be posted at every election station during voting hours and until the affidavit is completed.

3.2.8 After any election, a vote recount is prohibited. The fairness of the election must be guaranteed by strict adherence to electoral procedures. Alert partisan observers must contribute to the feeling of this universal fairness.

3.2.9 Donating money to candidates' Election Campaigns using credit cards is forbidden. Giving personal bank information, including the bank accounts to the election campaign or individual candidates is forbidden. Only checks, money orders and wire transfers initiated by the givers personally present at the banks are allowed.

3.2.10 Any elected official might be recalled by the electorate after a certain number of qualifying signatures is collected for the recall vote to occur. The recall vote might be conducted at any date of the year without waiting for the first Tuesday of November. The recall voting must be conducted using standard voting machines in secure environment with maximum protection against interference. Challenging the recall outcome is prohibited.

4 Ascertainment - certifying the election; Miscellaneous

4.1 The last Wednesday of November at 8:00 p.m. local time of the election year is the deadline for every state of the Union to certify the integrity of the Election, present the documentation to the Secretary of State and the State Supreme Court. The certification includes election of the state members of the U.S. House of Representatives, one of two state Senators representing the state in the Congress of the United States if their terms are about to expire and they ran for reelection and won, all Representatives to the State House and 1/3 of the state Senators. They also must certify votes cast for President and Vice-President of the United States in the leap years which would determine the number of electors the particular state will send to the Conference where the President and Vice-President will be elected. Votes for a variety of lesser elected positions must also be certified.

4.2 The U.S. Congress must be in session continuously through the year with the exception of the following periods:

- January -- New Year's Day, Jan 1st
- February -- A week starting at the Presidents' Day
- March -- A week in March in the middle of the month from Monday to Friday
- March or April - Two weeks of Easter Holiday, starting on the day after Palm Sunday.
- May – One week starting on Memorial Day
- July -- Two weeks starting on the July 3
- August -- A one month Summer Holiday beginning on August 10th
- Two days of Yom Kippur varies annually. If Yom Kippur falls on the weekend, the days off are shifted to the following week.

- October -- Two weeks starting on Columbus Day.
- November 11 -- Veteran's Day
- November -- Thanksgiving Week
- December -- Two weeks before the end of the year

During long time holidays the members of Congress must keep a reliable connection with the Government in Washington DC, with the stipulation that their return to the capital might be arranged instantly or their voting power could be used remotely in case of an emergency.

4.3 The terms of the President and Vice-President shall end at noon on the 3rd Wednesday of January of the year following the leap year, and the terms of some Senators and all Representatives at noon on the 1st Business Wednesday of January of odd years.

4.4 If at the time fixed for the beginning of the term of the President, the President elect has died, the Vice President elect shall become President. If the Vice-President dies, the President selects someone either from the pool of acting Governors, or member of Congress of the United States to serve as the Vice-President until the end of their vice-presidential term.

4.5 Vote counting must be performed by volunteers not associated with any commercial enterprise or political party with no criminal convictions in the background. Certified voting machines must be used.

5 - Membership, Rules, Journals, Adjournment

5.1 Preexisting U.S. Election Assistance Commission (EAC) is responsible for operating voting Systems for testing and certification of voting hardware and software. This EAC certifies, decertifies and recertifies voting system hardware and software and accredits test laboratories to assure the integrity of the voting process. The demonstration of flawless operations must be made visible to the public and members of the media a month before the elections.

5.2 Each House may determine the Rules of its Proceedings, punish its Members for Disorderly Behavior, and, with the concurrence of two-thirds of the Senate and simple majority in the House, expel a member through standard Impeachment and Trial procedures.

5.3 A carefully designed electronic communication system is necessary to document the voting pattern for every member of the House of Representative and the Senate. Although some issues might require temporary secrecy and must be withheld from publication, in general, publishing most of the proceedings and voting results is highly encouraged. That does not include personnel matters and impeachment voting which must be confidential.

5.4 Voting in Congress by proxy is prohibited. Absentee voting is allowed only in case of a serious illness or other clearly excusable circumstances and must be accomplished by presenting a signed and notarized voting document. Remote voting on a regular basis is prohibited.

6 - Compensation

6.1 The Senators and members of the House of Representatives must be compensated for their services at the annual rate equal to seven times the average annual income of the United States workers. Voting on personal compensation matters is prohibited.

6.2 Members of either house during their tenure have no right to occupy any paid position in commerce or public service other than the ones for which they have been elected.

7 - Bills, Legislative Process, Presidential Veto

7.1 Every Bill passed by the concurrence of the Senate and House of Representatives must be presented to the President of the United States for approval; if the President vetoes the bill the Senate and the House might reconsider it and schedule another vote. A vote resulting in 2/3rd of YES votes in both chambers in favor of the Bill is considered veto proof and automatically becomes Law thus overriding the President's veto.

7.2 Every Bill promulgated in the Congress must address one item only. The budget bill is considered addressing one item. Adding unrelated portions (Congressional Earmarks) is prohibited. Omnibus bills are prohibited. No bill, printed on paper, can exceed 100 pages typed in double space. Every member of Congress must read every word of the Bill they intend to sign and submit an affidavit to this effect with their clear signatures notarized. The same rule is applicable to the President of the United States.

8 Elective positions

8.1 Candidates for all elective positions, with the exception of lawyers running for nonpartisan judicial positions, must represent one of two parties, either Republican or Democratic Party and officially be endorsed by the party members through a Primaries Process. Running as Independent is not allowed with the exception of lawyers all of whom are considered running as independent. Lawyers can only run to fill judicial positions. All other political parties, although might be formed and organized, are not allowed to field candidates for any elective positions. Rejection of multiparty elections is based on history of the American electoral process which showed that independent candidates for President only siphoned votes from established political parties of Republicans and Democrats, drained financial resources of electorate and confused the electoral process.

8.2 Elective non-judicial positions include mayors of municipalities and counties, membership in city and county councils, members of the state's Senate and House of Representatives, state's Governor, state's Lieutenant Governor, United State Senate and House of Representatives, President and Vice President of the United States. Only people with roots in this country can run for the abovementioned positions if in addition they meet Intelligence Quotient testing requirements (IQ 130 and above for President and Vice-President, and 125 for all others), have a history of graduation from a four-year college with the exception of law school and also have a history of passing additional scientific tests specified in Appendix to this Constitution. Lawyers running for their elective positions do not take scientific tests. They must meet an Intelligence Quotient requirement of 120 or higher. An absolute requirement for any candidate is an absence of prior felony convictions, even if the candidate has been pardoned. In addition, the candidates for county's management positions, state's Senate and House of Representatives as well as Lieutenant Governor and Governor of the states cannot receive contributions from companies involved in urban or industrial development.

8.3 Individuals intended to run for any elective position must declare lack of commercial interests or investments with income or without, in any foreign country, for the previous five years, themselves, their family members and their in-laws, as well as any payments procured from foreign powers during the same period.

8.4 Only people with conventional sexuality (heterosexuals) are allowed to run for elective positions. Homosexual, bisexual, transgenders are not allowed to run for any elective position. People applying for election must document their conventional sexuality with a notarized statement. People who cannot satisfy all abovementioned requirements cannot run in the parties' primaries.

8.5 Individuals running for elective positions on County, and State levels cannot be themselves as well as their in-laws connected to any company involved in urban or industrial development.

8.6 On the floor of the Senate and the House of Representatives the members as well as guests are prohibited from making speeches longer than 30 minutes, however, presentations under questioning might exceed this limit.

8.7 Individuals just elected to elective positions or confirmed to occupy an assigned position, e.g., heads of the department, must take an Oath of Allegiance to the United States. The Oath must be articulated loudly while the individual places his dominant hand on the Judeo-Christian Bible. The individuals of Hebrew faith place their dominant hand on the Torah, should they choose so.

9 Assigned Top Positions

9.1 Directors of CIA, NSA, ATF, NASA and FDA must only be insiders, professionals working for the institutions in question for many years.

10.1 SUPREME COURT.

10.1 The Supreme Court of the United States (SCOTUS) consists of nine Justices, each serving a 10-year term. One justice is designated as the Chief Justice, the rest are associate justices. All nine justices have the right for one vote each. The Court is the Highest Court in the Federal Judiciary of the USA. It has ultimate appellate jurisdiction over all federal and state civil cases that involve a point of the federal law and *original jurisdiction* over the top echelon of federal servants of the USA including Ambassadors, Secretaries of the Departments and other public officials approved for their positions by the Senate of the United States. Court candidates must have years of experience in law at lower courts. When the Court has a vacancy open because of the resignation or death or expiration of the 10-year term of a particular justice, the qualified jurists might apply for positions to be considered by the Senate of the United States. Criminal cases are not subject to appeal and they therefore do not come to the attention of the Supreme Court or appellate courts of lower levels.

10.2 The Supreme Court does NOT have the right of Judicial Review.

10.3 The Constitution of 1788 has been hijacked by trial lawyers to use it as a tool for personal enrichment. The United States has wasted trillions of dollars to keep them afloat. An important role of the Constitution is to protect citizens from criminals, instead the 1788 Constitution is used to protect criminals from citizens. The New Constitution assumes that the best way for everyday and everyone's security is to sharply increase punishments for criminal offenses and limit the role of lawyers in the criminal justice system.

10.4 Exerting pressure on the Supreme Court or its individual members is prohibited.

11 No advertising for lawyers

11.1 Lawyers, paralegals, their family members, and in-laws are prohibited from contributing financially to any political party, party members or candidates for elective offices. Private lawyers are prohibited from advertising on TV, the Internet and through email, electronic texting, or physical ground or air, USPS, FedEx or UPS mail deliveries, or any innovations that might be available in the future. They are allowed to have a single informational page on the Internet describing their business in general. They are prohibited from recruiting clients for class action lawsuits or any other litigation.

11.2 The Food and Drug Administration's (FDA) approval indemnifies every new medication forever. Preexisting approvals by the FDA, given in the years past, to medications developed before this Constitution took effect, likewise, create legal umbrellas for medications in question. As long as new medications are approved by the FDA their developers receive immunity from legal actions by private lawyers, pertaining to the medication in question. When they lose their patent protection on expiration, the immunity continues to be valid even if the medications in question are subsequently manufactured as generic chemicals by different other manufacturers. The immunity continues even if the manufacturer withdrew the failed medication. The partial immunity is also extended to the practitioners using these medications. Malpractice litigation by private attorneys against medical practitioners can be initiated only with the official consent of either the American Medical Association or practitioners' specialty associations. Class action lawsuits pertaining to collegial medical practices and clinics, must be approved by the American Medical Association and the Justice Department. Lawsuits against manufacturers of medical products or medical devices must be approved by the American Academy of Pediatrics in case when the products or devices in question are aimed at children. Lawsuits against manufacturers of products and devices aimed at adults must be approved by the American Medical Association. Lawsuits against nursing homes and other long term as well as short term care facilities may be initiated only with the permission of the health departments of corresponding geographic administrative entities. Class action lawsuits outside the medical area are allowed only with the permission of the Justice Department and the Department of Commerce. Rejection of lawsuits by the above gatekeepers qualifies them as frivolous lawsuits. The above restrictions do not apply to Attorneys General of separate states. The U.S. Government and all organizations therein enjoy a broad liability protection against any potential lawsuits. The U.S. Government cannot be sued.

11.3 During criminal trials the defense lawyers are prohibited from making claims that their clients are mentally ill or had an episode of insanity, or were mentally unstable, or had stressful events in their past lives.

12 Elements of criminal code.

12.1 The American penal system, as described in this Constitution, is not based on humanitarian principles. The latter only encourage criminals and multiplies crimes, enriches trial lawyers and undermines peace. The new penal system is based on pragmatism.

12.2 College of Professional Jurors

12.2.1 The Justice Department (DOJ) creates and maintains a permanent College of Professional Jurors. The jurors are salaried from the budget of Department of Justice. The jurors might be individuals of either gender with roots in this country within the age limits between 23 and 70 and an IQ no less than 120. No individuals with felonies in their background might be admitted. They must have declared their sexual orientation. Only individuals with standard (dominant) sexual orientation (heterosexuals) are admitted to the College of Jurors. Individuals with gender conversion in their background are rejected. The jurors must be provided with means to save for their retirement, with the Justice Department contributing to their retirement funds. Thirteen jurors are randomly selected by the U.S. Department of Justice for every trial with the 13th juror being a substitute in case one of the12 jurors falls ill. Every deliberation is done by 12 jurors who are selected randomly by a computer program from the whole College of Jurors practicing country-wide, and notified no later than 10 days before the trial. The computer program used for selection must also keep both dates of each trial (beginning and the end) which is necessary for smooth selection process.

12.2.2 The airlines are obligated to provide the members of the College of Jurors with first class airplane tickets in violation of any waiting list for them to reach the location where their court session is scheduled to be. The jurors on the way to a trial must present a document to the airline confirming the fact that they are on an official business trip. The U.S. Department of Justice must cover the cost of the tickets. The Jurors' expense on meals and lodging must be likewise covered by the DOJ during the criminal or civil court sessions. Neither defense nor prosecution can question the jury selection or individual jurors.

12.2.3 Each juror must declare lack of historical personal contacts with the defendant or their kin. The jurors' presence at the trial is mandatory unless there are valid excusable circumstances. They are encouraged to familiarize themselves with the circumstances of the case before the trial. The prosecutors and defense have a right to present their witnesses. The number of witnesses cannot exceed 15 on each side. The guilty verdicts for every charge must be unanimous. If a jury cannot reach a unanimous verdict on a particular charge, the trial is dismissed and the suspect is retried with a different jury but the issues they consider are related to the only issues that were left at a disagreement by the first jury. If the second jury cannot reach a definitive verdict on the same charge, the charge is dropped and the defendant is called to be punished according to charges that passed either jury as "guilty." A defendant has a right to plead guilty to a certain charge, that plea cannot be withdrawn. The jury in this case does not consider the charge in question.

12.2.3 The jurors must be provided with all necessary attributes for a comfortable life during the trials and movements between them. Each juror must be given four weeks of paid vacation a year. Their annual salary must be ninefold of the average United States workers' salary.

There is no statute of limitation for any crime in the United States. If there is a chance of intimidation of the jurors, the jurors are arranged to watch the proceedings either from behind a curtain or via a set of closed TV systems. Attempts to threaten or intimidate professional jurors or witnesses are punishable by 25 years of prison confinement.

12.3 Grand Juries

12.3 Grand Juries must be composed of 21 citizens, recruited exclusively from voting areas, with individuals having documented IQ of at least 120. The individual requirements for them are the same as for College of Jurors. They must be compensated for the time they spend in deliberations. Any accusation or indictment requires consensus of 12 Grand Jurors. The deliberation by the Grand Jurors is conducted in complete secrecy. They are prohibited from publishing any information about the Grand Jury proceedings. Grand Juries possess a subpoena power.

13 Crime and punishment

Criminal investigations and trials:

13.1 Under the 1788 Constitution the prisons in many cases have become havens for criminals. Some individuals embedded with criminal culture commit crimes, even murders just to get to prison where all their dear friends are serving time. It is especially common in the black community. For many criminals the prisons are criminal universities. From the standpoint of the New Law, the New Constitution of the United States, an attempt to commit a crime equates to the crime executed. Criminal behavior is biological, genetic and does not depend on social conditions.

13.2 Potential degradation of the life of criminals, which the New Constitution advocates, is in the interest of every other citizen except the criminal lawyers.

13.3 *There is no punishment that is cruel or unusual. The Death penalty is neither cruel nor unusual. Self-incrimination if occurs is explicitly allowed and collected as evidence.*

13.4 Criminal investigations that might result in felonious charges are the responsibility of the lawyers at the local police departments, district, state and Federal attorneys or the Federal Bureau of Investigation (FBI) and Bureau of Alcohol, Tobacco and Firearms (ATF). The Police must use adequate profiling to better pinpoint potential suspects and this police activity cannot be challenged in the court of law. When the Police interact with a crime scene or simply monitor neighborhoods, they are encouraged to use ethnic and racial profiling, as well as considerations based on suspect's friends and relatives, statistics of crimes in the area, and other means potentially leading to solving cases expediently. The New Constitution rejects Miranda and the right to remain silent. There is no right to remain silent. Remaining silent might be held against the suspect in subsequent development of the case. In case the suspect requests a conversation with their lawyer, that opportunity must be given to them but the suspect must be held at a police station at the time of contact. Contacts via telephone are prohibited. Only personal contacts with the lawyers identifying themselves to the staff at the Police Station where the suspect is held are allowed. The contact lawyer must be carefully monitored. The lawyers cannot be paid from public funds. The suspects must be offered to plead guilty, not guilty or refuse to plead. In the second and third case the jury is convened, in the first case the jury is not convened and the Judge must proceed with sentencing. Plea withdrawal is not allowed.

13.5 During criminal murder or attempted murder investigations, the police have a right to name a suspect publicly in order to obtain their DNA (Deoxyribonucleic acid). In case of their refusal, individual suspects might be arrested and held in restraints in order to collect their DNA. Until the result of the DNA analysis is complete the individual suspects might be monitored with a GPS (Global Positioning System).

13.6 During the court hearing while presenting their arguments the prosecutors as well as the defense might present historical information concerning the accused behavior, their family and criminal history if available, and any relevant facts. Judges have no right to dismiss (toss out) any criminal case. No criminal case can be dismissed on "technicalities." Circumstances pertaining to prosecuting any criminal case must always be flexibly adjusted to run it to the logical conclusion.

13.7 The charges are formulated and rendered by the district, state, or federal attorneys. No negotiation with the defense is allowed. The charges might be withdrawn only by the office of the district or federal attorney before the trial under the pressure of new evidence only. The jury pronounces verdicts for every charge - guilty or not guilty. Alford plea is not allowed. The Presiding Judge then determines the punishment. The judges are not allowed to articulate any moralizations at the end of the criminal trials. The jury's decisions are final and cannot be overturned on technicalities. Probationary sentences are not allowed, all jury's verdicts (except not guilty) must result in either prison time or execution. The judges are allowed and indeed encouraged to increase, but not to decrease the severity of a sentence mandated by this Constitution, up to the death penalty, depending on circumstances. Suspended sentences, as well as "in lieu" sentences, are not allowed. Appeals to the higher court authority are not allowed in criminal cases.

13.8 Federal Judicial Districts will continue their existence as defined by the USA Judiciary by the year 2020: (11 Circuits plus a D.C. Circuit.)

13.9 Suspects are housed in jails until either conviction or a not guilty verdict on all counts. If not guilty, they are released. If found guilty they are immediately transferred to prison. No bails are allowed. All sentences are served in full, to a day; no releases on probation or parole or to halfway houses are allowed. The pretrial confinement in jail cannot exceed three months before a verdict is reached. For the extension of this time limit the court must petition the U.S. Department of Justice in cases of very complicated crime investigations. Insanity defense is not allowed. The pretrial detention in jail is subtracted from the time the individual must spend in prison. All suspects, found guilty, must serve their time in prison unless the sentence is capital punishment.

13.10 While in jails, the suspects must have access to their lawyers (if available), television broadcasting with current news, minimal but safe access to printed information. No public money could be spent on defense lawyers. Payment for defense is the responsibility of suspects themselves, their families, and charities. The defense lawyers must be members of the Bars of the corresponding states, and the number of defense lawyers for individual trials cannot exceed three. Any criminal trial may proceed without any defense lawyers whatsoever under the circumstances. In this case the suspect themselves is considered to be their own attorney. Smoking in jails for suspects and staff is prohibited.

13.11 Prisons are for confinement only. Multiple sentences are served consecutively and this practice cannot be changed by judges. Educational efforts, jobs training, psychological sessions, religious services, seminars of any kind, musical concerts, work activities, physical exercise on equipment bought for them by the taxpayers are all forbidden. No libraries are allowed to exist in the prison system. Especially dangerous inmates are kept separately with no access to the outside world. Volunteers are not allowed to enter the prisons. Prisons cannot entertain ideas of prisoners' rehabilitation. Prison inmates are not allowed to complain to any official organization. All Departments of Correction must be renamed Departments of Prisons. Prisoners are never paroled and must serve their sentences to the very end, except when they become old, infirm and demented whereas they are transferred to nursing homes. Brain biopsy is necessary to confirm the diagnosis of senile dementia in a prisoner. Smoking in prisons is prohibited for both the staff and the inmates.

13.12 Prisoners are not allowed to be transferred to local or remote hospitals under any circumstances. Outpatient visits by prisoners to outside clinics are forbidden. Inviting medical doctors-specialists to examine and possibly treat prisoners is banned. Admitting sick prisoners to state or private hospitals for inpatient treatment is banned. All illnesses that might otherwise require hospitalization must be treated at the prison infirmary. Instrumental (machine) hemodialysis on the prisoners on the prison territory or outside is forbidden. Simple peritoneal dialysis at the prison Infirmary is the only option. All surgical interventions must be performed at the prison infirmaries. Prisoners are not allowed any communication with the outside world. No written material including religious books, no television programs, nor functional telephone connections or access to the Internet are allowed. Finding an electronic communication device on a prisoner must be punished severely including increasing the time to be served and other administrative measures. All prisons are considered "no fly zones" by the FAA.

13.13 Communications with families and friends, visits by lawyers or relatives are forbidden for the prison inmates. A death in the family is not a reason for visitation. No special diet is allowed. All prisoners must have a standard diet with 1,800 calories daily. The food is given to prisoners twice a day, at 8:00 a.m. and 5:00 p.m. Only the simplest set of generic medications is allowed to be prescribed to the prisoners with an eye on maximizing savings. Brand name, recently developed advanced medications are prohibited to be used in the prisons. Prison riots are suppressed on the most expedient basis with minimal structural damage to the prison. The prisoners must be informed and advised that any violation may result in their severe punishment. The American society must accept the inevitable fact that life expectancy of the prisoners might be significantly lower than in citizens in a free society. The American society has no moral responsibility for the fact that prisoners put themselves at a disadvantage through their criminal behavior.

13.14 The prisons have complete, structurally built-in legal immunity indemnifying them, State Departments of Prisons, the States, the Federal Government, if the prison is Federal, from liability for whatever could happen to the prisoners. In many prisons the staff and some prisoners could have been former neighbors, went to the same school, played football together. It is the responsibility of the administrations to be aware of such situations of potential violation of the prisoners' regime, separate such prisoners and staff members to avoid any illegal contacts between them. Prisoner on prisoner violence is resolved only administratively, no outside lawyers are allowed to be involved. The preferred punishments are increasing the court mandated sentence and other measures suitable to the administration. Any prisoner escape is interpreted as an oversight/negligence by the prison administration and must result in firing the administrators and terminating their careers. In case of a prisoner's death, their body is cremated, family members if available are notified and the ashes are given to them.

13.15 Statute of Limitation for any crime never expires.

13.16 Death Penalty must be executed not later than one month after the sentence. No appeals or pleading by public figures are accepted. The method of execution is chosen by the prison staff.

13.17 Apprehensions of criminal suspects cannot be done "gently," they often develop in stressful situations, certain mortality outcome must be expected. It must always be assumed that untoward outcome of apprehension (in case of the suspect's death) is not the fault of the police force or other security establishment involved in the suspect's apprehension.

13.18 A moratorium must be imposed on any attempts by convicted criminals to profit from their notoriety through publications, movies, private donations, TV documentaries or lecturing.

13.19 Juvenile suspects are housed in jails in strict isolation from other suspects. After sentencing they are transferred to juvenal sections of local prisons with the same restrictions on their personal freedom as for the adult offenders, namely, no education, no entertainments, no contacts with family or lawyers and so on. After reaching age 18, if they still have time to serve, they are transferred to adult sections of the prisons. Juvenile suspects are treated as adults in terms of sentencing.

13.20 Criminal pursuit by the FBI and CIA but not by the foreign governments must be assisted by the technical companies if called for. Decoding manufactured communication devices might require their assistance. Refusal carries a punishment of seven years in prison.

13.21 The writ of Habeas Corpus is supported by the New Constitution.

13.22 INDUSTRIAL INCIDENTS

13.22 Criminal liability for industrial incidents falls on the shoulders of top management, including the Chief Executive Officers (CEOs) of the companies responsible for the incidents. Their claims of not awareness are considered "willful blindness" and are dismissed.

13.23 Losing information via insufficient IP networks protection

13.23 Individuals responsible for integrity and security of the local IP networks are CEOs and top managers of industrial corporations, hospitals, banks, security establishments and other organizations. Sufficient funds must be always allocated to defend local IP networks. Allowing foreign or domestic agents to breach IP networks through manifest negligence by administrators serving the abovementioned structures is punishable by a fine of $50,000 in 2020 U.S. dollars adjusted for inflation.

13.24 Downloading and / or installing communication software or hardware of foreign manufacture or ownership (e.g., Chinese, Russians) are all forbidden. Foreign communications applications made in communist or former communist countries present security risk.

13.25 Revealing the confidential U.S. government information to the World (leaks) in some cases exposes an obvious guilty party. If not, it creates a situation whereas the Justice Department has a right to identify possible suspects and demand their submission to a lie detector test. A suspect's refusal is interpreted as admission of guilt or as a guilty plea.

14 Preservation of values of special public properties.

14.1 Special Public Properties are historical monuments, including monuments honoring leaders of the Civil War on both sides of the conflict, streets and city blocks attracting foreign and American tourists, with real estate values exceeding averages for the cities. It is the responsibility of local and Federal Authorities to preserve value of those special places and guard them against vandals, domestic terrorists, vagabonds, transients and homeless, as well as ideologically poisoned young leftist crowds. Relocation of vagabonds to less desirable areas is the responsibility of the police.

14.2 Individuals caught in the process of destruction of special public properties are subject to arrest and a prison term of 20 years.

14.3 Private property cannot be taken for public use without fair compensation under any circumstances.

15 Illegal immigration

15.1 Illegal immigration, that is an attempt to cross the U.S. borders to enter the United States of America, without permission, constitutes a crime. Individuals involved in facilitation of illegal immigration are subject to punishment of 25 years in prison. No criminal or civil lawsuit can be initiated on behalf of illegal immigrants. Illegal immigrants are subject to being expelled from the country.

15.2 Illegal immigrants cannot be given a U.S. driver's license or any form of U.S. identification.

15.3 Public encampment by the homeless is prohibited.

16 Civil Trials

16.1 Civil Trials may be conducted as jury trials, as well as trials without a jury. In the latter case the decision is made by a judge or a group of three judges. In any case the judges must give a written, signed statement that they have no personal bias or a foregone conclusion in the case and would consider all the facts objectively. The signed statements must mention the sides in the dispute, as well as an indication if the judges have any financial benefits from the trial outcome (stocks, money, gifts) personally, their families or their in-laws. Such statements must be given under the penalty of perjury. Giving false information, if discovered, must result in the judge's impeachment, trial and subsequent criminal prosecution. Judges thus prosecuted are ineligible for pardon by governors or presidents of the United States. Trials involving foreign interests are especially suspicious for a possible bribe, gifts to judges, and must be scrutinized in detail by the Department of Justice. Security of the United States, leak of protected information, is a paramount consideration in such cases. It must also be considered that foreign influence might be channeled via a member of the judge's family or in-laws working in a foreign land where they might be bribed or simply influenced by a hostile power. This set of circumstances must come under consideration also in case if any judge becomes subject to confirmation or being elected to a new position.

16.2 When financial compensation to a victim is at stake in a trial, the lawyers' fee cannot exceed 7% of the settlement. In special trials of such nature both the lawyers and the judge(s) must give a written statement that they have no historical friendly contacts of any nature.

17 Criminality

17.1 Human behavior is genetically controlled. A large portion of crimes are genetically driven, which is evident from frequent appearance of blood related inmates in American prisons and probably in prisons worldwide. It is important for attorneys investigating serious crimes to dig into the family history and behavior, because quite often some family members were enablers for the criminal activity to occur. It is not necessary for prosecutors or lawyers describing facts in the case during deliberation to show that the suspect knew right from wrong.

17.2 It is mandatory for the U.S. Department of Justice as well as states' Attorneys General offices to organize sting operations for catching nonviolent criminals preying on innocent people in the Internet marketplace. An assumption is that such a system will complement other measures of crime prevention.

17.3 The Justice Department will maintain a database of all criminal cases in the United States where information on all convicted perpetrators, and their relatives is maintained with as much relevant information as possible, including DNA records. Family members of felons cannot refuse submitting their DNA under the penalty of freezing their bank accounts, confiscating their real estate properties and imposing financial fines.

17.4 Mass Shootings; events with mass casualties, mitigation and punishment.

Mass Shootings have become a serious threat to the American way of life. An effort must be made to seek out people with strange and antisocial behavior in specific geographical areas. To create such a list, police departments, neighborhood watch, adult and child protective services, delivery personnel and other socially active organizations with an intimate knowledge of their neighborhood should be contacted. Once such a list of "persons of interest" is formulated, a court order will be obtained and they would then be questioned by militia members. The next review of the case must include the search of their dwelling to determine if they possess weapons that may be used in such a crime and/or other evidence that a mass homicide is being contemplated. This will be accomplished after a Court Order is obtained. In the case that such weapons and evidence are found and, the person of interest is qualified as dangerous, the now suspect will be surveilled by local police (including internet searches) with the participation of a mental health criminal specialist.

Once it is determined that he is an imminent threat, the case goes to the court in order to enact Preemptive Incarceration.

The case would then go to the Grand Jury. If recommended for prosecution, the prosecutor will gather all documentation collected by the Militia and the case then proceeds to trial.

17.4 In case an episode of the mass shooting has taken place despite all precautions, after apprehension, mass shooters as well as individuals to have committed deadly crimes with moving vehicles, singular explosions or the like, resulting in multiple deaths or injury, must be placed in a secure prison immediately, bypassing the local jail. A Grand Jury must be convened immediately for the consideration of conviction. If a lawyer for the defendant is available, their attendance is arranged via a virtual presence only. The court hearing is done at the prison where the shooter is located. The jury must take the case no later than a month after the event. The punishment for mass shooting or any event with mass casualties is death. The death sentence is the only option for other events with mass mortality/injury with or without the actual usage of firearms. The FBI must interview the shooter's relatives and friends. If there is an indication that they inspired the shooter, after the Grand Jury decision, all relatives must also be prosecuted. In the event that law enforcement fails to mitigate the carnage of an active shooter, the officer or officers involved will be prosecuted to the fullest extent of the law, not to exclude life in prison. In conclusion, these mass shootings and bombings is a war on our way of life and should be approached as such.

COMPENSATION OF VICTIMS & BRAVE CITIZENS

The government will create a fund that is used to compensate the victims of mass shootings and other terrorist events that result in mass casualties. Compensation in the amount of $500,000 to $1.5 million will be determined by a special commission based on severity of injury. If the breadwinner of the family is killed or permanently disabled, a contracted insurance company will be consulted in order to access actuarial files to determine additional annual payments based on occupation and historical income. Prevention of Mass Shootings must rely on a special work by Militia Battalions. A fund will be established to reward citizens who show exceptional bravery for terminating the incident.

18 Considerations for punishing convicted criminals

This section of the Constitution describes selected criminal acts and appropriate punishment, the Constitution demands to be imposed for them. It is the responsibility of the U.S. Congress as well as the states' legislatures to complement this penal code with punishments for criminal activities omitted here. The expectation is that criminal acts not listed here will be met with commensurate punishment.

18.1 Death Penalty can be applied to convicted criminals aged 17 to 65. Individuals over 65 are not eligible for the death penalty. The maximum penalty of 50 years might be applied to criminals aged less than 17. Maximum penalty of 25 years might be applied to criminals aged 65 years and older. Mental Illness or altered mental state due to any illegal or therapeutic drugs or alcohol cannot be used as a defense.

18.2 The following activities are considered criminal and punishable by **capital punishment**.

- First- and Second-degree Murder
- Membership in a group involved in criminal activity; violent or non-violent gang membership.
- Participation in Organized Crime
- Kidnapping (family related kidnapping - statutory noncustodial kidnapping - is excluded)
- Disclosing confidential, secret information of the United States to hostile foreign entities or terrorist organizations.
- Any variety of Internet scam.
- Vehicular homicide.

18.3 **Natural Life in Prison** as a punishment for especially heinous crimes.

- Production of child pornography, purchasing a child for production of child pornography and possession of child pornography is punishable by life in prison.
- Health Care fraud
- Running a Ponzi Scheme
- Elder Fraud.

18.4 The following activities are considered criminal and punishable by the prison confinement of **35 years** duration

- Mining, creating or transacting in virtual (crypto) currencies
- Selling personal information of other individuals

- Advocating socialism, communism, anarchism or similar as a substitute for the capitalist system of the United States during an election campaign
- Advocating elements of the above, e.g., Federal Jobs
- guarantee, guaranteed income, guaranteed minimum wage
- Sexual offenses, Rape, sex with minors, underage sex
- Pimping, operating a prostitution ring
- Human trafficking; human smuggling across the U.S. borders
- Identity theft, creating new identities with criminal intent
- Operating Robocalls
- Money Laundering
- Any deceptive practice on the Internet, including circular references.
- Defacement of public lands or public monuments

18.5 The following crimes are punishable by 20 years in prison.

- Manufacture, distribution or selling marijuana, cannabinol, cannabidiol and related product.
- Distribution of illicit drugs or criminal information, including email addresses, telephones, people's addresses on the dark web, the Internet at large or through mail
- Adulteration of pharmaceuticals or food supply
- Selling or advertising fake vaccines or drugs with scientifically unsupported claims
- Stealing personal internet files and exposing them to the public

- Attempt to impose Sharia Law on the whole or a fraction of Society, including the Islamic groups in the United States
- Spreading unsolicited commercial messages (spam), emails sent with a criminal intent and phishing emails via electronic media. Sending robo calls with a criminal intent
- Deliberate blocking road traffic or creating impediment to procuring normal business operations (Equated to domestic terrorism. Not to be confused with traffic jams)
- Looting area businesses at the time of street riots
- Failure to prosecute individuals involved in public riots and looting
- illegally hunting wild protected animals.

18.6 The following criminal activities are punishable by 10 years in prison

- Driving under the influence
- Killing or torturing a companion animal
- Conspiracy to commit mail fraud; committing mail fraud
- Incitement to violence
- Charges of racism made in public against individuals or organizations
- Facilitation of illegal immigration
- Putting graffiti on the street walls
- Transporting for profit and trading in protected species
- Buying protected species for personal use
- Harassing public officials
- Stealing U.S. mail
- Targeted residential picketing

- Resisting arrest
- Falsification of IQ tests
- Blocking and Impeding movements of people or goods or services along critical infrastructures

Punishable by 10 years in prison with confiscation of equipment and $100,000 fine in 2020 dollars.

- Africanization of the United States. Africanization is defined as an act that makes the United States of America to become more identified with any African country or the African continent as a whole
- Latinization of the United States. Latinization is defined as an act that renders this country to become more identified with any of the Latin American countries
- Islamization of the United States. Islamization is defined as an act that renders this country more identified with any Islamic country, e.g., Syria or Afghanistan
- Criminalization of the United States. Criminalization is defined as taking or not taking certain measures that lead to, or could have been prevented, criminalization of society, spread criminal activity or giving "free hand" to criminals
- Cowardice in presence of mass shooting (pertaining to security guards and Police Force)

18.7 Every convicted prisoner might be allowed to speak for no longer than 15 minutes in court upon sentencing. Sentencing must be done no later than one week after the conviction. Every sentenced male prisoner must be surgically castrated upon admission to the prison by removing testicles to prevent prison violence as well as preventing perpetuating criminal genes in the next generation.

19 Street Violence (Domestic Riots)

19.1 Domestic riots have no justification under the law. They must be expediently suppressed by police, national guard or organized militias controlled by the Department of Homeland Security (DHS). Although batons, tear gas, pepper sprays or metal bullets with rubber coating or other nonlethal means are options to quell agitated crowds, any escalation of the violence by the crowd: setting objects on fire, throwing Molotov cocktails, igniting fireworks, breaking windows in private homes, in businesses or industrial buildings, destruction of transportation vehicles, robbing retail outlets, warrant using firearms with rapid fire capability. Helicopters are allowed to be used for riot suppression. Neither the State nor the Federal Government have any responsibility for consequences suffered by the rioters when crowd control is used. No civil or criminal lawsuit can be brought on behalf of individuals taking part in street riots and no monetary compensation can be offered to rioters or their kin suffering as a result. Individuals who mask their identity by obscuring their faces during street riots are considered the most dangerous and might be subjected to especially harsh treatment by the police or militias. Smash and grab thefts of retail stores are subject to suppression with automatic firearms with no liability attached to the property defenders. Targeted residential protests are prohibited. Burning the American Flag on the streets or in a public place constitutes a riot. Death of suspects with previous criminal convictions or without, in police custody cannot be litigated and paying settlements to the families of deceased is prohibited. Physical restraining individuals during arrest is considered holding them in police custody. Their death must always be ruled accidental or due to internal factors like substance abuse or a medical condition. A possibility is considered that residents of voting zones might cross into the area where riots occur in order to protect rioters. In this case, they are considered rioters themselves. Rioters relinquish their human rights and American Citizenship.

20 A look in the past: Destruction of American Cities and American Culture must be evaluated with a price tag attached

20.1 The Department of Commerce must form a Commission of Values Lost to Riots, whose responsibility is to provide estimates and put a dollar value on destructions of American real estate resulting from the street riots since 1950.

20.2 The Constitution condemns destruction of American monuments, including Civil War heroes' statues on both sides of the conflict. Such actions are criminal. The perpetrators have no grudge against the Civil War and their action constitutes perfect hooliganism. Cancel Culture is a combination of demagoguery and criminal actions.

DOMESTIC AFFAIRS

21 Religion

21.1 The attitude of the United States to World religions must be based on the principle of reciprocity. It is important to note that Christianity is persecuted in many Islamic countries. No Christianity is allowed in Saudi Arabia and Afghanistan for example.

21.2 The status of religion is therefore granted to Christianity, including both Catholic and Protestant denominations as well as Mormonism; Greek and East European Orthodox Christianity, Judaism (Hebrew), and Buddhism. All the rest of "religions" are deprived of this status including Islam, Scientology and various other small sects. They all must be taxed as profitable businesses at Federal, State and Local Levels.

21.3 The New Constitution reaffirms the principle of separation of church and state.

21.4 No exceptions from mandatory vaccinations ordered by the States or Federal Government can be given on religious grounds. The courts must reject any attempts to overturn them. Only certified medical exceptions are possible.

21.5 English is the official language of the United States. No other language could be used at state or Federal government institutions.

22 ADOPTIONS

22.1 Adoptions outside of biological families are prohibited. There must be biological genetic links between adopter and adoptee. Male homosexuals are forbidden from adopting children.

23 Armed Forces

23.1 Women do not serve in the Armed Forces with the exception of medical personnel in inland U.S. Army and Navy hospitals or Navy hospital ships. They can serve in Security Forces of the police, U.S. Customs and Border

Protection (CBP), the FBI and Secret Service. Women in the Police Force cannot be used in regular beats. They are there to deal preferentially with women law-breakers. Defense Secretary must be a civilian male individual. He cannot be a retired career military man. His paramount responsibility is furthering the strength of the United States Army, Navy, Marine Corps, Air Force and Space Force. He is prohibited from imposing left-wing or right-wing ideological concepts on the serving personnel. The President of the United States is the Commander-in-chief of the U.S. Armed Forces. If the President of the United States is a woman but the vice president is a man then the Vice-President becomes the commander in chief. The next group of elected officials who might be called to serve as the Commander-in-chief (individually) are the President of the Senate and the speaker of the House. Individuals with history of transgender transformation are prohibited from serving in the armed forces. All recruits, applicants to the military academies, must testify that they have normal or dominant sexual orientation, and are not homosexual and never had any gender conversion.

23.2 U.S. Army personnel as well as subcontractors are conferred an absolute immunity from prosecution while working in war zones overseas, with the exception of sexual crimes. The United States must resist any attempts by foreign or international legal bodies to indict American servicemen or U.S. Army subcontractors. Considering such actions of the foreign legal bodies as giving a helping hand to terrorism, the USA in such cases is encouraged to counter-indict judges of the well-known foreign states who have shown tendency to help terrorists worldwide. Bringing such judges to justice via Interpol or other routes is mandatory.

23.3 The U.S. Army must be neutral ideologically with no bias right or left. Attempts to impose left-wing or right-wing ideology on the Armed Forces are punishable by 25 years in prison. Only the American Flag might be displayed at military bases and institutions.

23.4 Creation of the American Foreign Legion is possible with the consent of the Congress of the United States. The Legion's Supreme Commander is the President of the United States or the vice-president in case the President is a woman. American Foreign Legion troops cannot be used on the territory of the United States, but can train here. They have complete legal immunity for their actions except for sexual crimes which are prosecuted by military courts. Membership might be open to foreign nationals from the following countries: Canada, Australia, New Zealand, South Korea, Japan, Spain, Portugal, Austria, Germany, Switzerland (German speaking part), England, Denmark, Netherlands, Norway, Sweden, Finland, Estonia, Poland, Israel and Greece. Only men are admitted with proven absence of criminal background. Their recompence is determined by the Department of Treasury. They must have a documented IQ of 105 or higher.

23.5 It is the responsibility of the President of the United States and the United States Congress to maintain an adequate military budget, to promote constant growth and strength of the United States Armed Forces. As long as we have adversaries in the world, the United States Armed Forces must remain strong. The history of neglect of the military budget by the United States Congress in the years prior to the Japanese attack on Pearl Harbor is a lesson that always must be kept in mind.

23.6 Military tribunals (Court-Martials). Jurisdiction for the court-martial encompasses both members of the United States military as well as the foreign subjects to have committed terrorist acts against the United States. The court consists of presiding Military Judge and 12 military jurors selected at random from a list of potential candidates in active service in the United States military. The jury must be composed of five officers, four NCO's and three privates. Decisions are "guilty" and "not guilty" and must be unanimous. The code is United States Civil Code. Military lawyer--advocate for the accused might be hired at the accused expense. If that cannot be done, a trial without a lawyer will proceed under the assumption that the accused acts as his own attorney. The first court decision is final and cannot be appealed. An interpreter may be hired at the accused's expense if the accused does not speak English.

23.7 Admissions to Military Academies is done based on recommendations of a member of the U.S. House of representatives or a U.S. Senator. Only young men are admitted. The applicant's parents must live in a voting zone and have roots in this country. Applicants must show good academic grades on entrance exams and an adequate score on the medical exam. Background in sports is a plus. They must sign a statement of their sexuality.

23.8 For the members of the Armed Forces with security clearance, contacts with the members of the press are prohibited without permission of the superior command. It is possible that an individual serving in the U.S. Army or another security organization has a family member or a close friend working for a media organization. In this case his supervisors must consider his transfer to a less problematic position in the security establishment. This latest rule is also applicable to any other individual working for an organization where security clearance is a prerequisite.

24 Education

24.1 Children with IQ below 95 are not admitted to public schools. Children of Islamic parents are not admitted to public schools and not educated at public expense. Children of Illegal immigrants cannot be educated at public expense. Special Education at public expense is prohibited. Segregated school systems are allowed. Busing is prohibited. Integrated Public schools are prohibited.

24.2 Promoting free education at college level at the expense of public money is forbidden. Quality education is a commodity and must be bought.

24.3 Admissions to the colleges and universities based on anything other than purely academic criteria are prohibited. Outside pressure on the universities to admit individuals with inadequate mental abilities (affirmative action) is prohibited. The IQ (or Scholastic Aptitude Test (SAT) score at high school graduation) of new applicants must lie not below the minus sigma deviation from the average IQ of the Normal Distribution of a students' IQ (mean) at a college or university in question. All applicants must present official certificates of their IQ and a certificate of the SAT score. The admissions are then based on their scores at high schools or GED (General Equivalency Diploma) and aptitude tests such as bona fide SAT and ACT, (American College Testing). Admitting to colleges individuals on sports scholarships is prohibited. Violation of the admission code described herein is punishable by depriving the school of financial grants and prosecution of the school administrators. The punishment is 15 years in prison for the school administrators.

24.4 One of the first acts under the New Constitution must be the evaluation of Individuals who have graduated from colleges and universities with the help of the affirmative actions and their performance in the workplace. Public disclosure of this information is mandatory.

24.5 Using race or ethnicity as a factor for admission (Affirmative Actions) to colleges and universities is declared illegal and punishable by 15 years of imprisonment. Charges formulated as a hate crime are prohibited.

24.6 Female participants in sport events, professionals or amateurs, must look female and be female biologically. If there are any doubts in the minds of some officials, they have a right to demand a hormone test and, in case the hormones in a particular individual do not match a standard female pattern, this participant must be rejected and expelled.

24.7 It is prohibited to teach Social and Political Sciences, sexual orientation to elementary, middle and high school students. Allowable subjects: English language, History of the United States and the World, Mathematics (algebra, geometry, trigonometry, math analysis), Physics, Chemistry, Geography, Biology, Astronomy, Anatomy of human and animal bodies, Music, Art, Housekeeping, Farming, Sports, Computers, Computer Programming, Foreign languages (French, Spanish, German, Russian, Chinese, Japanese). Teachers in elementary, middle and high schools must have a documented IQ of 107 or higher.

24.8 Practice of gender-affirmation for minors in public schools is prohibited.

24.9 Critical Race Theory is forbidden in public schools and universities that receive any public money. Practicing the above is punishable by five years of prison time.

24.10 The Department of Education must develop two standard curricula. (a) Curriculum with a techno-mathematical bend and (b) curriculum with humanitarian bend. Some subjects might intersect both curricula. Some students might prefer to graduate from a humanitarian track, others from a techno-mathematical track. The bifurcation of curricula must begin in high school. The American schools must prepare students for college and universities. Again, students with IQ below 95 are not admitted to public school and are not educated at public expense. The system of elective subjects will be complimentary to the system of suggested tracks.

25 Business

25.1 Excessive taxation of the rich is not a sound economic policy; it leads to spreading and multiplying governmental bureaucracy at the expense of productive forces that are suppressed. The rich are the backbone of the country like the United States. They are the ultimate source of innovation and technological progress as well as charitable actions and thus deserve respect. Rich businessmen and billionaires have built monumental medical facilities, Best in the World universities and other public structures. Left wingers who contribute nothing to the countries' prosperity do not hesitate to attack them. High taxation is a gift to American enemies. This country has always prospered with lower taxes. Taxing the rich on top of the regulatory income tax (wealth tax) is prohibited.

25.2 Lowering taxes is a sound economic policy as it enriches the state. Global or countrywide wealth redistribution is a foreign concept to this Constitution and is prohibited.

25.3 Any union vote, e.g., to organize a union or on personnel or policy matters must be done in secret without revealing the individual results which are then destroyed. Only the final results must be announced. The voting must be organized and controlled by a special committee established and approved by the Senate of the United States.

25.4 The new Constitution recognizes the Sherman Antitrust Act of 1890.

25.5 Companies and other institutions where the business model is admission of considerable fraction of the public to their premises have a right to establish their own dress code for visitors and staff and this dress code cannot be violated.

25.6 Global Minimum Corporate Tax Rate is not acceptable for the United States. Pay-Disclosure Laws are forbidden.

25.7 Food irradiation is the safest way to prevent spoilage, improve safety and quality of food.

25.8 The Government must minimize regulations.

26 Welfare, Public Health

26.1 Housing Assistance and Family and Children Assistance Programs are illegal in the United States and therefore prohibited. Any entitlement programs are prohibited.

26.2 Homeless veterans, honorably discharged must be offered multifaceted assistance in the area of housing, job training and health care.

26.3 Vaccinations prevent pandemics, national health emergencies and thus save lives and money. A vaccinated person is unlikely to infect other people, thus they are safe for society. Unvaccinated individuals might get infected from neighbors and spread infection around, putting many lives at risk. Someone might get sick and die because of another person's negligence. For individuals, who potentially might be a hot spot of infection, vaccinations are mandatory and refusal is punishable by a fine of $1,000 in 2020 dollars.

26.4 Daylight saving time must be permanent (all year round).

27 Militias

27.1 Militias are formed under the control and direction of Department of Homeland Security (DHS). Only men are admitted. Intelligent people with certain level of education are preferred. Retired military men might be candidates. Recruiters must monitor for radical right- and left-wing elements. The latter must be filtered out. The function of the militiamen is to control and suppress domestic rioting and criminal actions by the crowds. They might be used for pacification to suppress random shootings in high crime zones. They operate mostly in non-voting zones, during riots, although they might be used in supportive policing role in voting zones occupied by individuals blocking city traffic or disrupting other business functions. Their training is conducted in voting zones. Their bases are the local National Guard units, or Police Departments if the former are remote. They are entitled to specific uniform designed by the DHS and means of transportation including armored personnel carriers as well as the airplanes or helicopters when necessary. They must show maximum mobility during the riots. It is mandatory for them to have police style protective gear and automatic weapons. They are afforded absolute legal immunity during suppression of street riots or taking measures to prevent looting and destruction of property. Their supreme goal is to suppress rioting by any means. Mounted militias could be considered depending on circumstances. Using military personnel vehicles such as Stryker must be arranged per militia request. Militias must keep contact with local police and if the latter are in the militia way, militiamen have a right to demand the police clear the area.

27.2 Militias are temporary and may be disbanded any time depending on the presence or absence of street violence. While in service, Militia members are reimbursed at the rate of four times the average workers' salary in the United States. When available, the militias must be used preferentially before the Police step in. The police units must then be removed out of the area. Militia units must all undergo at least three weeks of specialized training before being used. Militiamen are organized in squads led by sergeants; squads are agglutinated in platoons led by militia lieutenants. The smallest operational unit might be a squad whereas one or two squads of a platoon will provide logistics and security, e.g., road closing to restrict access to the riot area. Militia units might be used in states other than the one they have been formed up. Militiamen are given titles of "public officials." Militia members are allowed and indeed encouraged to stop and frisk suspects under the threat of discharging firearms. They are also allowed to search the homes of the suspects. Every militiaman must have life insurance for $1,500,000 in 2020 money. The insurance must be bought and paid for them by the Department of Homeland Security. The DHS must maintain the insurance for as long as the militiamen are in service.

27.3 Within the circle of a two-mile radius in Washington DC, with the center of the circle on the White House, militias are controlled by the Secret Service.

28 FREEDOM OF THE PRESS

28.1 The United States Press is free by longstanding tradition. The government has no right to control the Internet, or publication of books or newspapers, production of movies, radio and television broadcast. The Congress has the responsibility to discourage political correctness in free press. People have the right to express their positive or negative views of their own and other races, their own ethnicity and other ethnicities and likewise it is prohibited from discouraging legitimate biological, psychometric and statistical research into racial differences without the fear of retribution. They also are free to express their political views. Enforcement of political correctness in public or private colleges and universities, government offices, editorial boards or publications with at least 2,000 readers or publicly traded companies is a criminal offense (felony) punishable by five years in prison and confiscation of all family property upon conviction.

28.2 Freedom of Speech and Freedom of the Press do not extend to publication of leaked classified government material. Leakage of classified government information is a high treason. Individuals responsible for the leak of classified government information are eligible for punishment between 25 years of prison time and the death penalty with confiscation of all family property upon conviction depending on the severity of the cases.

28.3 A single individual/family/company are prohibited from owning more than 10% of the American Media which includes newspapers, Internet equivalents, radio and television stations and broadcast companies. Owners of newspapers, movie studios, radio and television stations are prohibited from imposing ideological pressure on creative staff. The states and Federal Government are prohibited from dictating ideological directions to individuals and companies engaged in publishing.

29 Miscellaneous Prohibitions

Using private information channels for government propaganda is prohibited. The government is prohibited from shutting down private information channels. Affordable housing provisions are prohibited if construction thereof might lead to increase of criminality in the area. The decision makers who allowed the buildings must be held criminally responsible should this occur. Legislation of minimal wage and abortions are prohibited. Abortions cannot be a part of any United States Courts decisions or legislation initiative. They are allowed. Boy Scouts and Girl Scouts must be separate entities in recruitment and practice. Companies that do not produce any services or goods related to the patents they own (trolls) cannot own patents. Industrial projects of any kind on Federal Lands are prohibited with the exception of oil exploration and production in periods of petroleum crisis and high prices on the market. Using fur of farm animals, except cattle, for clothes design is prohibited. Transgender athletes cannot participate in girls or women's sports. Showing up in public dressed in Islamic garb is prohibited. Professional baseball, American football, soccer, basketball players and the administrators in the corresponding teams must have a documented IQ of at least 105. Government workers are prohibited from unionizing. Unionization cannot be supported or hindered by any State or Federal regulations. Paying ransom to criminal groups, hackers, kidnappers, terrorists is prohibited on a state, federal and personal level. College athletes are prohibited from unionizing. Paying government officials of any rank legal fees at taxpayer expense is prohibited while they are in office as well as after they quit or retired. Incorporated entities or individuals are prohibited from accumulating more than 12 family homes used for renting out. Affordable Care Act is banned. Manufacturing and exporting biomass from the United States is prohibited. Public drinking is prohibited. Disbanding or defunding police departments in the United States is prohibited unless for administrative reasons. Using the night vision devices during the hunting season is prohibited. Citizen arrests are illegal. Generating and selling Nonfungible Tokens (NFTs) is prohibited in the USA. Student loans could only be given to students entering colleges where they are likely to repay them after graduation. To assure this they must have an IQ not below of the minus sigma of the average IQ (mean) of students already to have graduated from the college in question. No title of nobility can be granted by the United States. No person in service of the United States can accept any gift of value without the explicit permission of the Congress. Imposing any duties on import or export is the privilege of the

Federal Government of the United States. Lawsuits against alleged "discrimination" in hiring or firing are prohibited. Such decisions belong to Administration that hires people. Union interventions in such matters are prohibited. Push for "diversity" is prohibited. Individuals working for businesses of strategic importance must have roots in this country. Individuals working for major manufacturers must have an IQ at least 105. No book can be censured or banned in the United States, unless it is child pornography. Transgender bathrooms are prohibited. Manufacturing single use plastic is forbidden. For candidates running for any elective office accepting money from foreign sources or money with questionable origin is forbidden and punishable by 10 years in prison. Street racing is prohibited. National Public Radio (NPR) is a biased information source serving one party only and funding it with the public funds is prohibited. Price control is prohibited.

Governments of the following countries are prohibited from posting messages on American social media: Russia, China, Belarus, Burma (Myanmar), Venezuela, Cuba and Nicaragua. Posting aimed at children is prohibited. Postings with sexual contents are banned.

American government offices, companies, universities and security establishments are prohibited from hiring individuals with roots in China or Russia if the institutions in question are involved in classified work.

Display of Nazi flags, uniforms, memorabilia as a challenge to American Citizens is banned and punishable by a monetary fine of USD50,000 in 2020 U.S. Currency. This fine must be imposed on every participant of the Nazi group involved in the incident in question. The history of WWII clearly showed that the Nazi party are enemies of the United

States, they had been bitten to the ground, and must be treated with contempt and heavy fines in the 21st Century.

30 Condemnation of the Left Wing

Criminality of the Left-Wing has long-standing historical roots worldwide. They usually start with sweet promises and those soon turn your life into economic ruins, suppression of freedom and terror. Examples of Communist Russia, China, Eastern Europe, Cuba, Venezuela and North Korea are good illustrations of the malignant pattern. In Russia and Eastern Europe, the citizens revolted and threw out the communist yoke. Very few want to go back. The New Constitution warns against supporting political left-wing promoters of socialism in this country. Socialism has a global stamp of oppression and hatred attached to it. The United States, the country American leftists hate, has served as a major attractor, a magnet for people in many countries, claiming they implemented socialism, socialism American leftists so much admire. Massive escapes from Cuba, Venezuela and Russia are well known. Such examples can be multiplied. "Democratic Socialism" is a fiction, deception by dishonest politicians, a lie. Attempts to impose left-wing norms on the American society is a crime punishable by 25 years in prison.

31 National Holidays

- New Year's Day January 1st
- Presidents Day (Washington's Birthday) - 3rd Monday of February
- Memorial Day - Last Monday in May
- Independence Day - July 4th.
- Labor Day - first Monday of September
- Columbus Day – October 12

- Veterans' Day November 11th
- Thanksgiving - 4th Thursday of November
- Christmas Day - December 25th

FOREIGN AFFAIRS

32 Independence of Democratic Taiwan must be guaranteed by American Naval Power and other means. Communist Dictatorship of China has no sovereignty over Independent and Democratic Taiwan.

33 Exposition of Islam

33.1 During WWII, North African Arabs spied for the Afrika Korps because of German persecution of Jews which resulted in some losses for the American troops. Hitler nurtured his connections with the Arab World. Palestinian Arabs celebrated and danced in the streets on September 11, 2001 in Gaza Strip as well as in the West Bank. American Muslims who include a sizable fraction of Palestinians also celebrated. Many young American Muslims joined the Islamic State. The Palestinians are therefore enemies of the United States. The United States therefore will never allow creation of the Palestinian State and will never negotiate prerequisites. No monetary funds will ever be allocated to the Palestinian Authority, Hamas or Gaza population. The Palestinians or their descendants cannot be permanent residents of the USA, cannot be U.S. citizens, cannot be admitted to American Universities, cannot study or teach in American Universities or serve in the U.S. Armed Forces, cannot be given security clearance to have access to classified work, cannot work at the Immigration and Naturalization Service or any other government departments. They cannot practice law in the United States. Islamic Quran is full of bloodthirsty messages aimed at non-Muslims: Tabari 9:69 "*Killing Unbelievers is a small matter to us,*" which is just one example. Islam presents an existential threat to the Unites States and all Western Civilization. During the takeover of Afghanistan in 2021 the Taliban pursued systematic search and killing of Christians. Islam begets violence. Armenian genocide is another bloody spot on the Muslim identity. Arabs, Muslims, contributed zero value to the development of the modern civilization historically.

33.2 The United States is committed to the support and protection of Israel and all Arab countries Israel maintains diplomatic relations with, in any eventuality. Jerusalem is the Capital of Israel. The Golan heights are a part of Israel. The United States recognizes that the future is unpredictable and the circumstances are subject to change, however, based on historical reality, the United States commits to protecting, through association and directly, the countries of English and German speaking people, in Europe, Australia and New Zealand, as well as non-Islamic countries of the rest of Western Europe, as well as Japan and South Korea. The United States pledges her support to the North Atlantic Treaty Organization (NATO). The United States must do everything to prevent migration of Africans to Europe, the United States of America, and Latin Americans to the United States and Canada. The United States must be vigilant about efforts by adversaries who hate our Constitutional Republic and try to undermine it. A significant portion of their efforts is being directed through the Internet. Islam, when combined with certain ethnicities, is an existential threat to the United States and the Western Civilization. It is an obligation to continually work for decreasing the footprint of Aggressive Islam on the World scene.

33.3 It is a responsibility of the United States Navy and the Air Force to enforce the freedom of navigation across the World waterways and airways, as well as protect marine mammals worldwide and all living creatures of the sea at risk of extinction.

34 Terrorism

34.1 Major responsibility of the Federal Government is to combat domestic and international terrorism. Killing terrorists in the field is the preferred method of their elimination. If caught, international terrorists once brought to justice are court marshalled by the military courts as soon as possible. The courts decisions are not subject to appeal. No civilian or military lawyers for the defense must be present. Negotiations with terrorists are prohibited. Under the New Constitution of the United States, terrorist suspects have no legal rights and must be treated to extermination. The task of dealing with terrorism control is delegated to the Armed Forces of the USA, security establishment of the United States: CIA, FBI, NSA and Drug Enforcement Administration. Pirates of the Sea are equated to terrorists. Membership in "*Moorish Sovereign Movement*" is punishable by 40 years in prison. No *sovereign organizations* independent of the Laws of the United States are allowed in this country. Any such claims are illegal and punishable by 40 years in prison.

34.2 The following ammunition and weapons are allowed to be used to fight foreign terrorists: napalm, tank-flamethrowers, fragmentation bombs and grenades, hollow point bullets, daisy cutters, fuel-air explosions (thermobaric weapons), cluster bombs, and any other weapons that are dictated by the strategic demands or tactical situations. The New Constitution does not recognize human shields typically used by terrorists.

35 ADDENDUM I

35.1 Structure of the Executive branch. List of the Departments of the Federal Government

- State
- Defense
- Treasure
- Justice. (The Justice Department must conduct itself as if it is independent from politics.)
- Interior
- Agriculture (USDA)
- Commerce
- Transportation
- Energy
- Education
- Homeland Security
- Veterans Affairs

35.2 The heads of the Departments are nominated by the President and approved by the Senate. They all must be individuals with roots in this county with IQ 120 or higher. The head of the Department of Justice (Attorney General) must be a lawyer and the head of the Department of Defense must be a man.

35.3 Responsibility of the Federal and State Governments:

- Protect young people using the Internet
- Provide safest environment abroad for American citizens through elimination of individual terrorists as well as rogue regimes hostile to the United States and her allies.

- Providing safest avenue for internal and international commerce through elimination of unfair commercial elements.
- Guarantee primacy of Environment protection over Development.
- Protecting the Privacy of citizens.
- Ensure competition between sources of information: newspapers, Internet Service Providers, cable television companies.
- Keep Inflation low
- Maintain the Armed Forces at a superbly alert level.

35.4 The Federal and State Governments cannot:

- Nationalize private lands, financial system or parts of the national enterprises.
- Establish a welfare state.

36 ADDENDUM II SCIENCE

36.1 The New American Constitution recognizes the following well established scientific facts. Our World (the Universe) was created via an event called the Big Bang approximately 13.7 billion years ago. The Universe is currently expanding at an accelerating rate. The size of the Universe is unknown, it may be infinite, but the visible Universe exceeds 80 billion light years across in any direction. The Earth and the Solar System are not the center of the Universe, the center of the Universe does not exist. A significant portion of the matter in the Universe (dark matter) is invisible. The stars congregate in galaxies (our Galaxy is the Milky Way) and the number of galaxies in the Visible Universe is at least 100 billion. The age of the solar system is five billion years, our Sun was therefore created at that time; the age of the planet

Earth is 4.5 billion years. The shape of the Earth is geoid which is flattened between the polar regions and expanded at the Equator because of the Earth rotation. Evolutionary theory of Charles Darwin is the only acceptable scientific theory explaining the multitude of species on the planet Earth, including humans. Humans (Homo Sapiens) evolved over a period of three to four million years, from a more primitive ape species. Non-avian dinosaurs roamed the earth last time 66 million years ago. Modern day birds are descendants of the avian dinosaurs. Global climate change (warming of the Earth atmosphere and world oceans) is an established fact, directly related to human industrial and agricultural activity. The United States Government and the whole society have an obligation to combat it. Intelligent Design is a wrong theory. The most effective means to fight epidemics is vaccination. It has been proven historically many times. Quantum Mechanics mathematically describes behavior of very small particles in the world around us, e.g., electrons. So called aliens have never visited the planet Earth because of enormous distances between the individual stars. Further investigation of the Universe and the search for possible new physics are still ongoing and a possibility exists that some corrections will eventually be made to the facts described in the above paragraph.

36.2 All candidates for high elective offices, as well as the heads of the departments of the Federal Government, must proclaim their understanding and acceptance of all above mentioned undeniable facts, supported by observations and what's more important – by mathematics. The Attorneys General are excluded.

36.3 The following scientific pursuits must be well funded and encouraged: Gene Editing, using fetal tissue for research.

37 WARNINGS:

37.4 Smoking tobacco causes lung and other cancers leading to premature death. The life expectancy of smokers is 15 years shorter on average than non-smokers. Advertising for tobacco in any media is prohibited.

37.5 Drinking any amount of alcohol damages the brain. Drinking vast amounts of alcohol is a slow suicide. Five percent of U.S. cancers are caused by alcohol. Alcohol also damages the heart. Advertising for alcohol in any media is prohibited.

38 ADDENDUM III. EMPLOYMENT

38.1 The hiring of new employees and the firing of the established ones are the sole responsibility of the Employer. Employer decisions cannot be challenged in court in the case of hiring or firing employees not fit for service or laying off employees under economic pressure. No outside pressure can be applied for the sake of diversity, equality or other ideological constructs. It is prohibited to mandate the composition of companies' board of directors for the sake of political diversity or equality. Promotion based exclusively on racial principle is prohibited, and punishable by 25 years in prison. Racial preferences of any kind in hiring are prohibited. The concept of the "racial justice" is foreign to this Constitution. People must be judged by their intelligence, achievements in education fields and previous work history. It is acceptable for employers to contact a new hire's previous place of work to get answers to pertinent questions.

38.2 Mishaps in production and exploitation.

Industrial mishaps decrease the reputation of the United States as Industrial power. Every such incident must be investigated by the Department of Commerce together with the Department of Energy and the Justice Department from the standpoint of appropriateness of the staff used. The New Constitution assumed that low quality people without sufficient intelligence could have been in crucial places when such incidents happen. The mentioned departments must demand investigation of IQ of people involved in industrial production or exploitation in places where such incidents happen even when such individuals have a history of IQ measured more than four years earlier. Results must be published.

39 ADDENDUM IV . Aberrant Sexual Deviations.

39.1 Upon enacting this Constitution all registered male sex offenders must be rounded up and castrated.

39.2 Homosexuality and bisexuality are genetically aberrant inheritable condition, not moral deviations. Homosexuals and bisexuals are recognized as having full rights with the following restrictions: they can serve neither in the Armed Forces nor any Governmental organization or in private industry where security clearance is required. Homosexuals are entitled to partnership agreements between themselves, but not same sex marriages. Their partners are not entitled to health benefits normally afforded to spouses. Homosexuals cannot run for elective offices in the United States. Homosexuals cannot be secretaries of the Government Departments of the United States. Homosexuals on the other hand have higher average intelligence than heterosexual individuals and their individual incomes are higher also. They especially succeed in visual and performing arts. Homosexuals worldwide have a lot in common and in fact constitute a separate ethnicity. German homosexuals have more in common with French homosexuals than with other Germans.

40 ADDENDUM V

District of Columbia remains a district and cannot be converted into a state or attached to the state of Maryland.

41 ADDENDUM VI

Federal Trade Commission (FTC) has a right to investigate illegal practices.

FTC is mandated to investigate putative fraudulent activities of companies dealing with U.S. consumers, and with other companies, as well as with the Government agencies with the purpose of seeking monetary relief for fraud victims (consumer redress) plus punitive damages. The FTC also has the right to seek court injunctions to stop fraudulent and deceptive commercial activity.

42 ADDENDUM VII. ARMENIAN GENOCIDE

The United States recognizes Armenian Genocide in 1915-1916 by the Turkish Government under the Ottoman Empire. Kurds, an Indo-European ethnicity, blackened their reputation forever by taking an active part in the events of 1915-1916, massacring thousands of Armenians. April 24, 2015 was the start of Armenian Genocide.

42 ADDENDUM VIII.

42.1 American amateur and professional athletes must show respect to the American Flag and the National Anthem. Acts of disrespecting American values are punishable by revoking their American Citizenship. Upon observing such incidents, they must be expelled from American sports organizations immediately. Showing disrespect to American symbols is not free speech.

42.2 Paying salaries to college athletes is prohibited.

43 ADDENDUM IX Investigations into public leaks

With the exception of the leaks, deliberately arranged by the Administration to probe public opinion on various issues, leaks of classified and confidential non-classified material constitute a crime. The procedure must start with someone making a list of possible suspects. The list then goes to the FBI who performs a lie-detector (polygraph) test on every individual. Those who failed get fired. Those who refused the test are fired also. Leaks of classified information must be tried in criminal court.

44 ADDENDUM X

TRANSITION PERIOD BETWEEN the TWO CONSTITUTIONS. Scenario (Duration - Two years or less)

44.1 Under certain circumstances, the President might be recognized as being incompetent to serve as President by a panel of physicians from Walter Reed Medical Center.

44.2 A Survey is conducted among presumed voting areas about the attitude of the population toward the New Constitution and in case of unquestionable acceptance the next phase is enacted.

44.3 A Chief Executive Officer (CEO) is installed in the White House after both the President and Vice-President resign. The New Constitution is going to be effected immediately, although it might still be the subject of corrections by the Constitutional Convention. Militia contingents are recruited. Members of the College of Jurors are recruited. The U.S. Congress and the Supreme Court stop functioning. The Election Commission establishes the election procedure for the Constitutional Convention. The election of members for the Constitutional Convention is conducted in the shortest possible time with two representatives from each state and one representative from the District of Columbia.

44.4 The Constitutional Convention is located in the building currently occupied by the U.S. House of Representatives. The Constitutional Assembly (Convention) begins to discuss the draft of the new Constitution and do necessary editing. The Constitution is then offered for voting to the residents of the voting zones. After the voting, if approved, the Constitution is signed by the members of the Constitutional Assembly who represent the voting population of their respective states. The election of new members of Congress, state governors, state Supreme Courts and the U.S. Supreme Court as well as the President and Vice President are announced and the campaign begins. State and Federal legislators, State Governors, Lieutenant Governor and the President and Vice-President of the United States as well as the members of the New U.S. Supreme Court as well as State Supreme Courts are elected and assume their respective offices.

45 Amendments

45.1 Future amendments must be promulgated as newly projected laws by both chambers of the U.S. Congress with a two third majority. Prospective Amendments thereafter must be sent to the States and approved by legislations of all 50 states. After that the prospective Amendment becomes a law and a part of the Constitution.

45.2 The New Constitution will be eligible for amendments after 50 years.

46 Appendix

Exams of scientific knowledge for public officials.

46.1 The exams must be developed by a special commission under the control of the American Academy of Sciences. The examination must be conducted by answering multiple choice and Yes-No questions. The tests are not intended to reveal deep practical working knowledge but rather familiarity with subjects constituting description of the structure of our Universe and its dynamics. The knowledge of applications of mathematics to natural phenomena is of the utmost importance at the exams. The questions themselves and answers to them must be kept for 10 years for every individual.

- Elementary Math: algebra, geometry, trigonometry
- Mathematical Analysis, real and complex analysis, ordinary and partial differential equations. Vector and Matrix calculus, Probability theory, Statistics
- Physics, including general familiarity with quantum mechanics and relativity theories

- Organic, Inorganic and physical Chemistry
- Cosmology, creation of the Universe, the Sun and the Earth, Evolution of the planet Earth; Earth Science, origin of life on Earth
- Anthropology, Biology, Evolution of Species
- Ecology
- Constitution of the United States
- History of the United States
- Recent history of major International Players, some of whom present economic challenge to the United States: China, Russia, France, Germany, Iran, Saudi Arabia, India, Brazil, Argentina, and Chili

46.2 The examination of the solicitors of public offices must consist of a 3-day examination with six hours every day of multiple choice or yes-no questions. Passing score is 75%. The Constitution expects that booklets will be published to help solicitors of public offices in the above examinations.

THE END

Written on behalf of the American People by Dr. Alex Blaivas

www.ingramcontent.com/pod-product-compliance
Lightning Source LLC
LaVergne TN
LVHW091120150826
845673LV00002B/903

* 9 7 9 8 8 4 5 9 4 8 4 7 2 *